APPLIED MATH SKILLS

Percents

CAMBRIDGE ADULT EDUCATION
A Division of Simon & Schuster
Upper Saddle River, New Jersey

Executive Editor: Mark Moscowitz
Market Manager: Will Jarred
Project Editors: Karen Bernhaut, Douglas Falk, Amy Jolin, Kristin Shepos-Salvatore
Editorial Development: Pat Cusick & Associates
Production Editors: Alan Dalgleish, John Roberts
Interior Design and Electronic Page Production: Lesiak/Crampton Design, Inc.
Cover Design: Pat Smythe

Printed in the United States of America

1 2 3 4 5 6 7 8 9 10   99 98 97 96 95

ISBN 0-835-94629-0

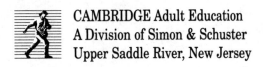

CAMBRIDGE Adult Education
A Division of Simon & Schuster
Upper Saddle River, New Jersey

CONTENTS

CHAPTER 1 Introduction to Percent

LESSON 1	Parts of a Whole: Fractions, Decimals, and Percent	1
LESSON 2	The Meaning of Percent	5
LESSON 3	Changing Between Decimals and Percent	10
LESSON 4	Changing Fractions to Percent	13
LESSON 5	Percent Larger Than 100%	16
LESSON 6	Percent Smaller Than 1%	20
CHAPTER 1	Summary	24
CHAPTER 1	MATH AT WORK	27

CHAPTER 2 Percent Applications

LESSON 7	Finding Commissions	31
LESSON 8	Percent of Increase	34
LESSON 9	Percent of Decrease	38
LESSON 10	Pie Graphs and Bar Graphs	42
LESSON 11	Using Information from Graphs	47
CHAPTER 2	Summary	51
CHAPTER 2	MATH AT WORK	53

CHAPTER 3 The Part, the Whole, the Percent

LESSON 12	Finding Part of a Number	57
LESSON 13	Finding a Number from its Percent	60
LESSON 14	Finding the Original Price	63
LESSON 15	Finding Percent from Part and Whole	66
LESSON 16	Applying Proportion to Percent Problems	69
CHAPTER 3	Summary	73
CHAPTER 3	MATH AT WORK	75

CHAPTER 4 Interest

LESSON 17	The Meaning of Simple Interest	79
LESSON 18	Simple Interest for More Than a Year	83
LESSON 19	Simple Interest for Less Than a Year	86
LESSON 20	Compound Interest	89
CHAPTER 4	Summary	93
CHAPTER 4	MATH AT WORK	95

ANSWER KEY ... 99

TO THE LEARNER

The books in the Applied Math series are designed to help you understand and practice math skills. Lessons are easy to use, and the problems demonstrate how math is used in the workplace.

Lessons have the following features:

- Every lesson is based on a problem encountered in the workplace. You are asked to use your knowledge of math to find a solution.

- The *Words to Know* sections introduce you to important terms and symbols as you begin each lesson.

- The *Example* sections show you how to use the skills presented in the lesson. The *Example* shows each step of the problem and gives you an easy-to-read explanation of the computation process.

- The *Exercise* sections give you a chance to practice new math skills gained from the *Example*. Every *Exercise* includes an *Application* question that allows you to use these skills in a new workplace problem.

- The *Math Tip* sections provide summaries, suggestions, alternative problem-solving strategies, and aids to help you remember and apply selected skills from the lessons.

- The *Use What You Have Learned* sections review all the math introduced the lesson's *Examples*. The *Applications* combine new skills with skills previously learned to solve problems drawn from a variety of workplaces.

Each chapter of each book contains a *Summary* and *Math at Work* section to help you judge how well you have mastered the chapter's material. The *Summary* reviews the math skills taught in the preceding chapter. *Math at Work* contains workplace problems that require the learner to use all of the skills taught to that point in the book. The *Answer Key* section at the end of the book provides answers, worked-out solutions, and explanations of how the problems can be solved. Answers are printed in color to make them easy to find. Use the worked-out solutions to see where errors occurred or to compare your successful approach to a problem with the author's.

The lessons in this book are designed to help you gain increased confidence in your math skills and to show you the practical value of mathematics in your working life. Good luck.

CHAPTER 1

Introduction to Percent

LESSON 1 Parts of a Whole: Fractions, Decimals, and Percent

Words to **KNOW**

A **percent** is a fraction or ratio with 100 as the denominator. If you are successful 9 out of 12 times, you are successful 75% of time. The ratio of 9 to 12 is equivalent to the ratio of 75 to 100. When you say that you are successful 75 percent of the time, you are saying that you succeed 75 out of each 100 times you try. The symbol for percent is **%**, and the word can be spelled either percent or per cent.

Reynaldo is in charge of packing at a Christmas ornament manufacturer. He gets a call from his supervisor. Reynaldo's supervisor has just received a complaint from a customer. One hundred twenty-five of the five thousand boxes of ornaments that the customer received contained at least one broken bulb. Reynaldo's supervisor asks him to reship one hundred and twenty-five boxes and to see if there is a problem with the packing operation.

Reynaldo's department has just begun to use foam packing inserts to separate the glass globes in twelve-packs of ornaments. Last year they used cardboard dividers. Reynaldo goes to his records and finds that, of the 425,000 boxes of bulbs shipped last year, 11,000 needed to be replaced due to breakage. Reynaldo needs to determine how 125 out of 5,000 compares to 11,000 out of 425,000.

Reynaldo first looks at the two figures as fractions. He isn't satisfied that he can really understand how the ratios compare with the numbers in this form.

current	*last year*
$\dfrac{125}{5,000}$	$\dfrac{11,000}{425,000}$

Then he gets his calculator and converts the fractions into decimals. $11,000 \div 425,000$ equals .0258823. $125 \div 5,000$ equals .003. Then he rounds these to thousandths. The decimal for breakage using the old cardboard inserts is .026. The decimal for breakage using the new inserts is .003.

current	*last year*
	(.025883)
.003	.026
× 100	× 100
0.3	2.6
0.3%	2.6%

To Reynaldo, this means that there is really no problem. He sees that the breakage in the current shipment is far less than the breakage they had experienced with the old inserts. But, he wants to make sure he can convince his supervisor. So, before he calls his supervisor, he does one more step. He multiplies both his decimal fractions by one hundred. By doing this, he can call his supervisor and say, "There doesn't seem to be a problem. Last year, our breakage was running at about 2.6 **percent**. The breakage on this last shipment was about 0.3 **percent**. Before, more than 2 boxes out of one hundred got broken. Now we have less than one out of one hundred being broken. It looks like the new inserts are doing a much better job."

Fractions, Decimals, and Percent

Like fractions and decimals, **percent** is a way to compare a part of something to an overall total. One hundred percent (100%) is all of something. It is equivalent to the decimal 1.0 or any fraction where the numerator and denominator are equal (i.e.: $\frac{2}{2}$, $\frac{5}{5}$, $\frac{17}{17}$).

EXAMPLE 1

Equivalent fractions, decimals, and percent

Look at the following chart of fractional equivalence. It shows the relationship among commonly used proper fractions, decimals, and percents. Decimals are rounded to the nearest thousandth, and the percents are rounded to the nearest whole percent.

Fractions	Decimals	Percent
1/2	.5	50%
1/4	.25	25%
3/4	.75	75%
1/3	.333	33%
2/3	.667	67%
1/8	.125	13%
3/8	.375	38%
5/8	.625	63%
7/8	.875	88%
1/5	.2	20%
2/5	.4	40%
3/5	.6	60%
4/5	.8	80%

EXERCISE 1

APPLICATIONS

Use the chart above to answer the following questions.

1. Martha has been late for work three times in the last year (250 days). The company wide rate for tardiness is 2.3%. Is Martha late more often than most workers?

   yes or no

2. Bryon's stamping machine is turning out four rejected parts out of every run of one thousand. When a machine's reject rate exceeds 3%, the machine is shut down for recalibration. Is it time for Byron to shut down his machine?

   yes or no

3. Bill completed $\frac{1}{5}$ of his monthly quota during the first week of the month. Melanie completed 23% of her quota during the first week. Who completed the larger part of their quota, Melanie or Bill?

4. $\frac{1}{10}$ of something is the equivalent of 10%. $\frac{2}{10}$ is 20%. What is the percent equivalent of:

   $\frac{3}{10}$? $\frac{5}{10}$? $\frac{7}{10}$? $\frac{9}{10}$?

Check your answers
on page 99.

USE WHAT YOU HAVE LEARNED

Circle the largest member of each of the following groups.

1. $\frac{1}{3}$ .437   44%

2. $\frac{2}{3}$ .654   66%

3. $\frac{2}{5}$ .42   40%

4. $\frac{3}{4}$ .875   .88%

Circle the two values in each group that are equal.

5. $\frac{2}{5}$ .4   4%

6. $\frac{4}{2}$ .4200   42%

7. $\frac{5}{8}$ .625   58%

8. $\frac{4}{5}$ .45   80%

9. Rochelle works as a flight attendant for New World Airlines. Last year, 3 out of 4 flights she was on arrived on time. This year, she is arriving on time 70% of the time. Does the airline's on-time performance seem to be improving?

yes or no

10. Dan is a waiter. He averages $375 a week in earnings. $125 of this $375 is salary and the rest is tips. Does his salary represent more than 25% of his income?

yes or no

11. Sonia is the assistant manager of a hotel. A company planning to use the hotel for a convention asked her to block out 150 rooms for the dates of the convention. 50% of the rooms were to be single occupancy, and the rest were to be double occupancy. By the end of the registration closing date, 85 people had asked to reserve single rooms. Had Sonia set aside enough single occupancy rooms?

yes or no

12. Brad is a nurse. There are three other nurses on his floor. They are each supposed to take care of 25% of the rooms on the floor. Brad has been assigned 6 of the 20 rooms. Has Brad been assigned the proper number of rooms, or does he have more than or less than he is supposed to have?

13. Brett is a teacher. His contract says that he is guaranteed 15% of his time every day for preparation. He works 8 hours a day, and gets 1 hour after lunch for class preparation. Is he getting the correct amount of preparation time guaranteed, or is he getting more than or less than he is supposed to have?

14. Nina is building a wheel chair ramp on the side of a building. A variance allows her to construct a 14% grade. The grade is based on a fraction with the height of the ramp as the numerator and the length of the ramp as the denominator. The ramp is 2 feet high and 16 feet long. Is the grade of the ramp more or less than 14%?

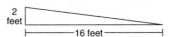

Check your answers on page 99.

LESSON 2   The Meaning of Percent

The whole is a number of something. The **whole** is the number that would supply the denominator if you chose to express the relationship as a fraction.

The **part** is also a number of something. The part is the number that would supply the numerator if you chose to express the relationship as a fraction.

The **percent** is the decimal equivalent of the fraction describing the ratio between the part and the whole multiplied by 100.

Bonnie is trying to judge the performance of two different stores. Both have sold more merchandise this year than last year.

Sales at the Brandywine location went from $231,000 in 1994 to $285,000 in 1995. During the same two years, sales at the Newport location went from $86,000 to $118,000.

It is obvious that the Brandywine location had larger sales overall ($285,000 to $118,000), and that it enjoyed a larger increase in sales ($54,000 to $32,000). However, the Newport store is much smaller and has fewer employees. It is a different-sized operation, and Bonnie is interested in comparing the performance of the two stores in a more even way. She decides to look at the percent of improvement that each store enjoyed.

The Uses of Percent

Percent is a way of expressing fractions in terms of "how many out of one hundred." This allows you to compare groups of items of greatly different size.

EXAMPLE 1

By what percent did each store improve?

Step 1 First, Bonnie creates a fraction based on each store's performance of the previous year and the amount of increase that each recorded. You see these fractions on the right.

Newport	*Brandywine*
$\dfrac{32,000}{86,000}$	$\dfrac{54,000}{231,000}$

Step 2 Then she converts these two fractions into decimals. Bonnie rounds both decimals to the nearest thousandth.

$$\frac{32,000}{86.000} = .372093$$

$$\frac{54,000}{285,000} = .1894736$$

Step 3 Now that Bonnie has her decimal equivalents, she converts these to percents by multiplying both decimals by one hundred.

(.372093)	(.1894736)
.372	.189
× 100	× 100
37.2	18.9
37%	19%

Bonnie finds that sales increased at the Newport store by a little more than 37% and at the Brandywine store by not quite 19%. This doesn't mean that the Newport store took in more money. It means that, for every $100 in sales the it made in the previous year, the Newport store made $137 this year. The Brandywine store sold only $19 per one hundred dollars more than last year. It means that, as a percent of total sales, the Newport store improved more than the Brandywine store.

EXERCISE 2A

APPLICATIONS

1. Shift 1 had 400 defects out of 6,000 nozzles produced. Shift 2 had 200 defects out of 5,000 nozzles produced. Which shift had the highest percent of defects?

2. Joey works for the highway department. He places machines along streets and highways that count numbers of cars using the road. In 1992, Joey's measurement of a certain stretch of road showed an average of 6,000 cars per day passed by his counter. In 1995, traffic on the same stretch of road had increased by 3,000 cars to 9,000 cars per day. Is this increase closer to 5%, 50%, or 500%?

Check your answers on page 100.

Percent, Part, and Whole

There are three parts in every expression of percent: The percent, the part, and the whole.

EXAMPLE 2

15 is what percent of 25?

Bonnie receives a trial shipment of 25 blouses from a new supplier. The shipment contains 5 small, 15 medium, and 5 large blouses. This will be typical of the shipments she will receive in the future. She wants to know the percent of medium blouses she can expect each shipment.

Step 1   Bonnie finds the percent of the trial shipment by using her information as you see at right. The part of the shipment she is interested in is the 15 medium blouses from the whole shipment of 25. 60% of each shipment will be medium.

$$\textbf{part} = 15$$
$$\textbf{whole} = 25$$
$$15 \div 25 = 0.6$$

$$0.6 \times 100 = 60\%$$

$$\text{part} \div \text{whole} = \text{percent}$$

Step 2 To find the number of medium blouses in the next shipment, Bonnie must rearrange her information. She knows the size of the whole order (200) and the percent of the medium blouses in the order, but needs the number for the medium sized part of the order. Using the decimal equivalent of the percent, she multiplies. 120 blouses will be medium.

$$whole = 200$$
$$percent = 60\% \ (0.6)$$

$$200 \times 0.6 = 120$$

$$whole \times percent = part$$

Step 3 Bonnie needs 210 medium blouses to stock all of her stores. She wants to know how large an order (the whole) she needs to make for the medium part to be 210 blouses. To find the whole, she divides the part (210) by the percent (.6). She needs to order 350 blouses to get the 210 she needs.

$$part = 210$$
$$percent = 60\% \ (0.6)$$

$$210 \div 0.6 = 350$$

$$part \div percent = whole$$

Much of this book is devoted to showing you how to recognize and use the relationship between these three values.

EXERCISE 2B

3. Stephanie works at an airline reservation counter. Checking the 2:30 flight to Portland, she saw that 114 of 120 seats had been booked. This means the plane is filled to 95% of capacity.

   Which of the values described above represents the *part*?

   Which of the values described above represents the *whole*?

   Which of the values described above represents the *percent*?

4. Karen has applied for a government job that stipulates that she agree to travel up to 30% of her working time. If she works 250 days per year, this means that she could travel as many as 75 days out of the year.

   Which of the values described above represents the *part*?

   Which of the values described above represents the *whole*?

   Which of the values described above represents the *percent*?

APPLICATION

5. On another stretch of road, Joey finds that the traffic has increased by twelve hundred cars per day between 1992 and 1995. What additional piece of information do you need in order to determine the percent of increase in traffic for this stretch of road?

Is this missing information the whole or the part?

Check your answers on page 100.

You will see the relationship between percent, part, and whole used in three different ways:

part ÷ whole = percent

whole × percent = part

part ÷ percent = whole

Percent problems require that you know two of the values, so that you can determine the third.

USE WHAT YOU HAVE LEARNED

APPLICATIONS

Identify the part, whole, and percent in each of the following problems.

1. Virginia manages the South Hills Inn. She finds that 65% of her 106 rooms are booked for Saturday. How many rooms are booked?

   As described above, is 65% the part, the whole, or the percent?

   As described above, is 106 rooms the part, the whole, or the percent?

   As described above, is the missing information the part, the whole, or the percent?

2. A customer gives Joe a 40% coupon to pay for a picture frame. With the coupon, the frame costs $64.80. What was the original cost of the frame?

   As described above, is 40% the part, the whole, or the percent?

   As described above, is $64.80 the part, the whole, or the percent?

   As described above, is the missing information the part, the whole, or the percent?

3. Elaine is a member of an office supply warehouse shopping club. She pays $59.60 for $65.50 worth of supplies. What is Elaine's percent of savings?

As described above, is $59.60 the part, the whole, or the percent?

As described above, is $65.60 the part, the whole, or the percent?

As described above, is the missing information the part, the whole, or the percent?

4. Clayton earns a take-home salary of $1,928 each month after 25% of his earnings are deducted for benefit payments and taxes. What is Clayton's total salary each month?

As described above, is $1,928 the part, the whole, or the percent?

As described above, is 25% the part, the whole, or the percent?

As described above, is the missing information the part, the whole, or the percent?

5. Carl's store advertises a computer for $1,600. He sells it for $1,400. The sale price is what percent of the advertised price?

As described above, is $1,600 the part, the whole, or the percent?

As described above, is $1,400 the part, the whole, or the percent?

As described above, is the missing information the part, the whole, or the percent?

6. Twelve of Betty's employees are full time. This is 60% of her employees. How many employees work for Betty?

As described above, is 60% the part, the whole, or the percent?

As described above, is 12 employees the part, the whole, or the percent?

As described, is the missing information the part, the whole, or the percent?

Check your answers on page 100.

LESSON 3 Changing Between Decimals and Percent

Sonia is the assistant manager for a hotel. She was told that next weekend, 25% of the rooms will be reserved for a convention. The hotel has a total of 852 rooms. How many of these rooms should she reserve? To make this calculation, Sonia must first convert the 25% into a decimal.

Converting Percent to Decimals

To find out how many rooms she needs to reserve, Sonia must convert by dividing the percent value, 25, by 100.

$$25 \div 100 = 0.25$$

$$
\begin{array}{r}
852 \\
\times\ .25 \\
\hline
4260 \\
17040 \\
\hline
213.00
\end{array}
$$

She now can multiply this decimal value by the total, which gives her the number of rooms to reserve.

Percent is a way of expressing "how many out of one hundred." Convert percents into decimals by multiplying the percent by .01 or by dividing the percent by 100. Both of these methods call on you to move the decimal point in the percent two places to the left.

EXAMPLE 1

Change 45% into a decimal.

Step 1 Set up the problem with the percent value.   **45%**

Step 2 Move the decimal point two places to the left. This is the decimal.   **45%**

0.45

EXERCISE 3A

Convert each example into a decimal.

1. 84%   2. 45%   3. 13%   4. 5%

APPLICATION

Check your answers on page 101.

5. Sonia was also told to give the guests attending the convention a 15% discount. To find the discount, what number should she multiply with the price?

Converting Decimals to Percent

If you have a decimal and need to know what percent it is, you simply multiply the decimal by 100. This means you move the decimal point two places to the right.

EXAMPLE 2

What percent is 0.99?

Step 1	Set up the problem.	.99
Step 2	Move the decimal point two places to the right. Add the percent sign.	.99.
		99%

EXERCISE 3B

What is the percent value of the following decimals?

6. 0.12   7. 0.68   8. 0.75   9. 0.01

APPLICATION

10. Sonia wants to know what percent of the rooms are already booked for next weekend. She calculated that 0.91 of their rooms are already booked. What percent is this?

Check your answers on page 101.

When converting from percent to decimals, always move the decimal point two places to the left. When converting from decimals to percent, always move the decimal point two places to the right.

USE WHAT YOU HAVE LEARNED

Change the following percents into decimals.

1. 89%   2. 40%   3. 92%   4. 3%

Change the following decimals into percent.

5. 0.79   6. 0.32   7. 0.07   8. 0.53

APPLICATIONS

9. Eduardo works in a clothes store. It is the end of summer, and the store is having a clearance sale, with 30% off all summer merchandise. To find the discount, what number should he multiply with the price?

10. Laura is the head of the marketing department. She was told to reduce the marketing budget. She calculated the amount to be 0.08 of her original budget. What percent will she have to cut?

11. Sheryl sells digital pagers. She earns 35% of her total sales and gets a $50 bonus for each complete package that she sells. She sold $7,500.00 last month including two complete packages. How much will she earn?

12. Demetrius is the sales manager for Discount Futons. He got the figures for last year's sales. He calculates that the most popular model made up 0.49 of last year's sales. What percent is this? The second best selling item made up .23 percent of last years sales. What percent is this?

13. Sonia was told that the hotel has 5% of the 855 rooms left for tomorrow night. How many rooms are available?

14. Harold wants to compare his company's profits from this year with last year. Last year his profits were about $350,000.00. He predicts that this year's profits will be $400,000.00. What percent of last year's profits is this increase?

Check your answers on page 101.

LESSON 4   Changing Fractions to Percent

Dan is a waiter. Tonight he made $57 in tips and $15 in hourly wages. His total earnings were $72. He wants to know what percent his hourly wages were of his total earnings. To figure this out, Dan must first create a fraction, and then convert the fraction into a percent.

Converting Fractions to Percent

Words to **KNOW**

When working with percents and fractions, the **numerator** is usually called the **part** and the **denominator** is called the **whole**.

To find out what percent his hourly wage is of his total earnings, Dan first needs a fraction. The **numerator**, or the **part**, will be his hourly wage, and the **denominator**, or the **whole**, will be his total earnings.

$$\frac{15}{72} \quad \frac{\text{part}}{\text{whole}}$$

Dan already knows that his hourly wage makes up $15 of his $72 total earnings. A percent will tell him what part his hourly wage plays in each $100 he makes.

$$\frac{15}{72} = \frac{?}{100}$$

To change the fraction to a percent, Dan first needs to convert the fraction into a decimal, and then convert that decimal into a percent.

$$\frac{15}{72} = 0.208$$

$$20.8\%$$

To change the fraction to a decimal, divide the part by the whole.

To change the decimal to a percent, move the decimal point over two places to the right.

EXAMPLE 1

What percent is $\frac{18}{23}$?

Step 1   Set up the problem.

$$\frac{18}{23}$$

Step 2   Convert the fraction into a decimal.

$$\frac{18}{23} = 0.783$$

Step 3   Convert the decimal into a percent.

$$0.783 = 78.3\%$$

EXERCISE 4

Change the following fractions into percents.

1. $\frac{4}{9}$ 2. $\frac{13}{25}$ 3. $\frac{31}{115}$ 4. $\frac{127}{349}$

APPLICATION

5. At the end of the two week period, Dan gets his paycheck. He has earned about $65 in hourly wage in addition to about $290 in tips. This time, he wants to know what percent his hourly wage is over the two week period. What are his total earnings, and what percent of that is his hourly wage?

Check your answers on page 102.

To change a fraction to a percent, always change the fraction to a decimal first, and then change the decimal to a percent.

USE WHAT YOU HAVE LEARNED

Change the following fractions to percents.

1. $\dfrac{5}{9}$

2. $\dfrac{3}{7}$

3. $\dfrac{8}{27}$

4. $\dfrac{3}{61}$

5. $\dfrac{12}{91}$

6. $\dfrac{26}{73}$

7. $\dfrac{57}{283}$

8. $\dfrac{139}{765}$

APPLICATIONS

9. On the following night, Dan made about $47 in tips. He is always supposed to tip the busboy about 2% of his own tips. He gives the busboy a dollar. Is this enough?

10. Barbara runs a small business making gift baskets. She sells each basket for $29.00. The cost of materials for each basket is $10.00. What percent profit ($29.00 - $10.00) does she make for each basket?

11. Barbara was looking over her figures from last year. She sold a total of 1,528 baskets. 639 of these were sold within the two weeks before Christmas, and 467 were sold shortly before Mother's Day. What percent of her total number of baskets sold were for the Christmas season? What percent were sold for Mother's day?

12. Scott is the receiving clerk for a gift shop. A shipment of ornaments has come in, and he finds that 26 out of the 500 ornaments are damaged. What percent of the ornaments are damaged?

13. Alan is a mechanic. He noticed that his expenses have gone up by about 1%. To make up for the rising costs, he plans to raise the price for an oil change from $12.95 to $14.95. Will this be enough to make up for his added expenses?

14. Kendra paints and sells T-shirts. Last week she sold 52 shirts. She needs to order more plain shirts and wants to know how many of each size to order. 3 of the 52 shirts that she sold were size small, 10 were medium, 19 were large, and 20 were extra large. What percent of the total did she sell of each size? If she orders 200 shirts, how many of each size should she order?

Check your answers on page 102.

LESSON 5   Percent Larger Than 100%

Rochelle works for New World Airlines. She pulls up the reservations for this afternoon's flight to Charleston and sees that it is 105% full. This means that the flight is overbooked. In the same way that airlines can overbook flights, percent can be greater than 100%. In this case, the "part" is larger than the "whole." If the airplane can hold 120 passengers, how many people have reservations?

Changing Percent to Decimals

To find out how many people have reservations, Rochelle converts the percent into a decimal by moving the decimal point two places to the right and multiplying.

EXAMPLE 1

What is 105% of 120?

Step 1	Set up the problem.	$105\% = 105.0$
Step 2	Move the decimal point two places to the left.	$1.05.0$
Step 3	Multiply the "whole" by the decimal.	

$$\begin{array}{r} 120 \\ \times 1.05 \\ \hline 600 \\ 12000 \\ \hline 126.00 \end{array}$$

EXERCISE 5A

Change the following percents to decimals.

1. 129%   **2.** 590%   **3.** 234%   **4.** 101%

APPLICATION

5. Rochelle looks at the next flight to Charleston and sees that it is also overbooked. This flight has a maximum capacity of 150 passengers, but it is 103% full. How many people have reservations for this flight?

Check your answers on page 103.

Changing Decimals to Percent

To change decimals greater than one to percents, follow the same procedure as with decimals smaller than one.

EXAMPLE 2

Change 1.46 to a percent.

Step 1 Set up the problem.   1.46

Step 2 Move the decimal point two places to the right.   1.46.

                                                                    146%

EXERCISE 5B

Change the following decimals to percent.

6. 5.29   **7.** 2.93   **8.** 3.67   **9.** 8.36

APPLICATION

10. Rochelle has checked all the passengers in for the afternoon flight. She calculates that there are about 1.02 passengers for every available seat, so she has to ask for volunteers to take another flight. What percent of the plane is booked?

Check your answers on page 103.

Changing Fractions to Percent

To change fractions greater than one to percent, follow the same procedure as with fractions less than one.

EXAMPLE 3

Change $3\frac{6}{7}$ to a percent.

Step 1 Set up the problem. $3\frac{6}{7}$

Step 2 Change the fraction into a decimal by dividing the numerator by the denominator. $3\frac{6}{7} = 3.857$

Step 3 Change the decimal into a percent by moving the decimal point two places to the right. $3.85.7 = 385.7\%$

EXERCISE 5C

Change the following fractions into percent.

11. $4\frac{1}{2}$ 12. $1\frac{2}{3}$ 13. $9\frac{9}{10}$ 14. $2\frac{3}{4}$

APPLICATION

15. Rochelle had two volunteers to take the next flight to Charleston. This means that there are 138 reservations for a flight that can carry 130 passengers. By what percent is the flight overbooked?

Check your answers on page 103.

Even if the percent is more than one hundred, do all calculations in the same way as with percents less than one hundred.

USE WHAT YOU HAVE LEARNED

Change the following percents into decimals.

1. 405%   2. 120%   3. 238%   4. 672%

Change the following decimals to percents.

5. 1.49   6. 8.99   7. 7.51   8. 9.11

Change the following fractions into percents.

9. $2\frac{4}{5}$ 10. $5\frac{4}{9}$ 11. $8\frac{2}{3}$ 12. $6\frac{1}{9}$

APPLICATIONS

13. Russ works in a feed store. He has poured about 11 pounds of seed into a bin that is supposed to hold 10 pounds of seed. What percent of the bin is full?

14. Gina works for a landscaping company. Her boss told her that she ordered too much fertilizer. In fact, she ordered 150% of what they actually needed. She should have ordered 50 bags. How many bags did she order?

15. Jerome makes and sells bookcases from his home. He has 12 standard bookcases in stock, but he received an order for 15 bookcases. What percent of his stock is this?

16. Jerome sells each bookcase for $30.00. If it costs him $10.00 for the materials to make a bookcase, then the price is what percent of the cost of materials?

17. Amanda is the manager of a gift shop. On an average day, the store makes $1,349.00 in profit. Today the store made $2,193.00 in profit. What percent of the average figures were today's profits?

18. Earl is in charge of a banquet hall. Next weekend, there will be a large banquet, and 685 people are expected to attend. The maximum capacity of the banquet hall is 600 people. What percent of maximum capacity is the scheduled banquet?

Check your answers on page 103.

LESSON 6 Percent Smaller Than 1%

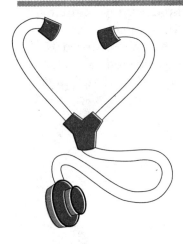

Brad is a nurse. He received a phone call from a concerned patient. She had heard that her son's vaccination for the measles has only a 99.99% reliability. This means that 0.01%, or one out of every hundred people who have this vaccination actually get the measles. What should Brad say to the patient?

Changing Percent to Decimals

To show the patient how small 0.01% actually is, Brad converts the percent into a decimal. This is done in the same way as with percent larger than 1%.

EXAMPLE 1

Change 0.01% to a decimal.

Step 1 Set up the problem. 　　　　　　　　　　　　　　0.01

Step 2 Move the decimal point two places to the left. 　　0.00.01

Brad explained to the patient that 0.01% is equal to 0.0001, which means that one out of every 10,000 people gets the measles from the vaccination. This is a much smaller number than one out of every 100.

EXERCISE 6A

Change the following percents to decimals.

1. 0.5%　　　　　2. 0.09%　　　　　3. 0.16%　　　　　4. 0.021%

APPLICATION

5. Brad received another phone call from a patient who asked about his routine tests having a 0.1% failure rate. The patient thought that the test failed one out of ten times. What should Brad tell this patient? How often does the test actually fail?

Check your answers
on page 104.

Changing Decimals to Percent

To change a decimal to a percent, follow the same procedure as with decimals larger than 0.01.

EXAMPLE 2

Change 0.0006 to a percent.

Step 1	Set up the problem.	0.0006
Step 2	Move the decimal point two places to the right.	0.00.06 = 0.06%

EXERCISE 6B

Change the following decimals to percent.

6. 0.007   **7.** 0.0071   **8.** 0.0003   **9.** 0.00038

APPLICATION

10. Brad looked at his records and saw that the newest vaccination available has a success rate of 0.9999. What is the failure rate? What percent of all vaccinations may fail?

Check your answers on page 104.

Changing Fractions to Percent

To change fractions less than $\frac{1}{100}$ to percents, follow the same procedure as with fractions greater than $\frac{1}{100}$.

EXAMPLE 3

Change $\frac{1}{890}$ to a percent.

Step 1	Set up the problem.	$\frac{1}{890}$
Step 2	Change the fraction to a decimal by dividing.	$1 \div 890 = 0.0011$
Step 3	Change the decimal to a percent by moving the decimal point two places to the right.	0.00.11 = 0.11%

EXERCISE 6C

Change the following fractions to percent.

11. $\dfrac{2}{984}$　　　　12. $\dfrac{11}{12,937}$　　　13. $\dfrac{3}{682}$　　　　14. $\dfrac{27}{15,835}$

APPLICATION

15. Brad knows there were 3 people who have contracted the flu after being vaccinated this year. The records show that the clinic has vaccinated 11,254 people. What percent of the vaccinations failed?

Check your answers on page 104.

Even if the percent is smaller than one, do all calculations as if it were larger than one.

USE WHAT YOU HAVE LEARNED

Change the following percents to decimals.

1. 0.8%　　　　　　2. 0.08%　　　　　　3. 0.019%　　　　　4. 0.71%

Change the following decimals to percent.

5. 0.0005　　　　　6. 0.005　　　　　　7. 0.00026　　　　　8. 0.0026

Change the following fractions to percent.

9. $\dfrac{1}{999}$　　　　10. $\dfrac{18}{9,157}$　　　　11. $\dfrac{29}{9,782}$　　　　12. $\dfrac{327}{98,644}$

APPLICATIONS

13. Chelsea works for a glassware company. She spoke to a client who received a shipment with 4 broken glasses. The shipment contained 5,000 glasses. What percent of the glasses in the shipment were broken?

14. Charles is in charge of quality control at a soft drink company. Federal regulations permit one part per hundred thousand of impure substances. What percent of a given beverage would this be?

15. Caroline sells alarm systems. The most popular package has a failure rate of 0.03%. How can she make this number sound more appealing to the customer? How often would the customer expect the alarm system to fail?

16. Howard is in charge of the mailings for a market research company. Last week he mailed out 1,500 questionnaires. This week, 21 of them were returned because the addressee had moved. What percent of the mailing was returned?

17. Kevin works at a printing shop. He finished an order for 5,124 copies, and found that four of the copies are flawed. What percent of the total is this? How many flawed copies could he expect to have in 15,000 copies?

18. Melanie develops photographs. The machine that she uses has ruined 3 photographs out of the past 850. What percent is this? When the machine starts ruining 1% of the photographs, her supervisor will have it repaired. How many more bad photographs would she have needed to have the machine repaired?

Check your answers on page 105.

CHAPTER 1 Summary

Fractions, Decimals, and Percent

Like and decimals, percent is a way to compare a part of something to an overall total. One hundred percent (100%) is all of something. It is equivalent to the decimal 1.0 or any fraction where the numerator and denominator are equal (i.e.: $\frac{2}{2}$, $\frac{5}{5}$, $\frac{17}{17}$).

The following chart lists equivalent fractions, decimals, and percent.

Fractions	Decimals	Percent
1/2	.5	50%
1/4	.25	25%
3/4	.75	75%
1/3	.333	33%
2/3	.667	67%
1/8	.125	13%
3/8	.375	38%
5/8	.625	63%
7/8	.875	88%
1/5	.2	20%
2/5	.4	40%
3/5	.6	60%
4/5	.8	80%

EXERCISE A

Circle the smallest member of each of the following sets.

1. $\frac{1}{4}$ .25   14%

2. $\frac{1}{3}$ .3   33%

3. $\frac{3}{5}$ .8   80%

4. $\frac{3}{10}$ .3   .3%

Check your answers on page 106.

The Percent, the Part, and the Whole

The whole is a number of something. The whole is the number that would be the denominator if you chose to express the relationship as a fraction. The part is also a number of something. The part is the number that would be the numerator if you chose to express the relationship as a fraction. The percent is 100 times the decimal equivalent of the ratio between the part and the whole.

EXERCISE B

APPLICATION

5. Norman has completed 72 wiring inspections. This is 60% of the 120 inspections he has scheduled for the month.

   Which of the values described above represents the part?

   Which of the values described above represents the whole?

   Which of the values described above represents the percent?

Check your answers on page 106.

Converting Percents and Decimals

Convert percents into decimals by multiplying the percent by .01 or by dividing it by 100. Both these methods call on you to move the decimal point in the percent two places to the left.

EXERCISE C

Convert each example into a decimal.

6. 84%   7. 45%   8. 13%   9. 5%

Check your answers on page 106.

Converting Fractions into Percent

To change a fraction to a decimal, simply divide the numerator (part) by the denominator (whole). Multiply the decimal quotient times 100.

EXERCISE D

Change the following fractions into percent.

10. $\dfrac{5}{8}$ 11. $\dfrac{11}{33}$ 12. $\dfrac{56}{64}$ 13. $\dfrac{72}{108}$

Check your answers
on page 106.

Percent Greater Than 100% and Less Than 1%

Percent can be greater than 100% and less than 1%. When you compute a decimal, remember that whole percent begins in the hundredths place. If the decimal is a mixed decimal, then the percent is greater than 100%. Values in decimals to the right of the hundredths place represent fractions of percent.

EXERCISE E

Convert the following into percent.

14. 1.03   15. .0013   16. 3.034   17. $\dfrac{25}{20}$

Check your answers
on page 106.

MATH AT WORK

1. **Marketing Director** Laura, head of the marketing department, has been told to decrease her $145,000 budget by $50,000. What percent of her budget does this represent?

2. **Salesperson** Sharon earns 25% of all her sales on digital pagers and complete packages including equipment and service. She also earns a $50 bonus for each complete package. She sold $8,250 last month and three complete packages. How much did she earn?

3. **Sales Manager** Deiter, sales manager for a beer importing company, learns that .34 of his gross sales were Mexican beers, .48 in German beers, and .18 in British ales. What percents do these sales represent? If his total sales were $250,500, how much of each type was sold?

4. **Horticulturist** Franz, a florist, reviewed his sales figures for last year. He sold 723 baskets before Christmas and 455 before Mother's Day. What percent of the total baskets sold were sold at Christmas? What percent were sold at Mother's Day?

5. **Shipping Clerk** Scott, who works in the shipping department of Santa's Elves' Gift Company, found that 286 ornaments of 10,000 ornaments shipped were broken. What percent were broken?

6. **Shipping Clerk** If each of the ornaments Scott inventories is worth $2.95, how much money do the damaged goods represent?

MATH AT WORK

7. Receiving Clerk   Russ is checking a new shipment. Although the 100 bolts of canvas were ordered, 111 were delivered. What percent was over-shipped?

8. Receiving Clerk   Russ also found that although the company had ordered 85 cases of assorted colored thread, only 82 were delivered. What percent was missing?

9. Fashion Buyer   Anne, a buyer for Baltman's department store, notices that one of the boxes of dresses sustained water damage during shipping. 35 of the 5,000 dresses in the order were damaged. What percent were damaged?

10. Travel Agent   Happy Trails Travel Agency has booked a 200-room hotel for a convention. This represents 50 single rooms, 120 doubles, and 30 suites. One week before the group was scheduled to arrive, reservations with deposits accounted for 32 singles, 12 suites and 89 doubles. What percent of each type of accommodations were full? What percent of the hotel was not yet booked?

11. Accountant   Mary's supervisor said that sales were down by one eighth this year. Since she knew the company's sales were $740,000 last year, what were the sales for this year?

12. Messenger   Dan earns $1,500 per month as a messenger and pays $300 in taxes. What fractional part of his wages go to taxes? What percent is this?

13. **Marketer**   Sarah manages the mailing list for a large marketing company. Her last mailing went out to 40,000 customers. 32 pieces of mail were returned. What was the percent of return?

14. **Salesperson**   Don generally makes $1,200 in commission each month. This month he made $1,800. What percent of his average commission did he make this month?

15. **Public Relations Representative**   The new baseball stadium can hold 50,000 fans. 56,000 tickets were sold for the opening game. What percent of maximum capacity was sold?

16. **Printer**   Kevin works at Quick-Print. After completing a job of 3,500 collated copies, he notices that 7 were wrinkled when coming out of the printer. What percent were flawed? On that basis, how many would be flawed on a 15,000 print job?

17. **Photographic Technician**   Melanie develops photographs in a 24-hour photo developer. She notices that 4 pictures were ruined in yesterday's run of 880. When the machine ruins .4% of pictures, she must call for service. Should she call for service?

18. **Entrepreneur**   Jenny's goal is to double sales in her craft store by the end of the year. Last year her sales were $5,550. This year, at the end of September, her sales were at $8,350. What percent ahead of last year is she, and how much more will she have to sell to meet her goal?

MATH AT WORK

19. **Sales Manager** Discount Futons had a sale where they sold $10,750 worth of merchandise for $8,062.50. What percent discount was offered?

20. **Truck Driver** Ed's old truck got 15 miles to the gallon, so, with a 10-gallon tank, he could drive 150 miles for deliveries. His new truck gets 22 miles to the gallon. How much further can he travel on one 10-gallon tank of gas, and what percent of the old truck's distance does this represent?

21. **Hotel Manager** Sonia has just informed the manager that only 3% of the hotel's 210 rooms are vacant for the coming weekend. He told her to add 10% to this figure to account for people who wouldn't make their reservations. How many rooms are likely be available for the weekend?

22. **Personnel Representative** Three-fourths of Tad's company enrolled in the company health plan. Of this group, .7 opted to join a health maintenance organization (HMO). If there are 2,452 employees, then what percent joined HMOs?

23. **Real Estate Agent** John received a $7\frac{1}{2}\%$ commission for selling a piece of land for $33,500.00. How much money did he receive?

24. **Salesperson** Jay's commission rate as a new distributor of health care products was half of his supervisor's commission rate. If his supervisor sold $25,050 worth of product and received $12,525 commission, how much will Jay make if he sells $4,350 worth of retail products?

Check your answers on page 107.

30   Chapter 1   Introduction to Percent

CHAPTER 2

Percent Applications

LESSON 7   Finding Commissions

Words to **KNOW**

Commissions are usually paid to salespersons and are calculated as a percent of sales. The **rate of commission** is a percent that describes the part of the sales price that the salesman is to receive.

Ramon is a real estate agent. He receives a **commission** for every house he sells.

Finding Commissions

Commission is found by multiplying the price of an object or service by a **rate of commission.**

Ramon sold a house for $84,500. He receives a 3% commission for this sale. To determine the amount of his commission, Ramon multiplies the price of the house by the commission rate.

EXAMPLE 1

84,500 x 3%

Step 1   Change the percent to a decimal:
3% = .03.

Step 2   Multiply the sales amount by the percent:
$84,500 × .03 = $2,535.

$$\begin{array}{r} 84{,}500 \\ \times .03 \\ \hline 2{,}535.00 \end{array}$$

EXERCISE 7

Find the commission.

1. a 5% commission rate on a sale of $980

2. a 25% commission rate on a sale of $12,300

3. a 4% commission rate on a sale of $68,600

4. a 20% commission rate on a sale of $570

Check your answers
on page 109.

APPLICATION

5. Ramon sold another home for $63,900. If he receives a 3% commission for this sale, then how much commission did he make?

 When finding commission, multiply the sales price by the commission rate.

USE WHAT YOU HAVE LEARNED

Find the commission.

1. a 7% commission rate on a sale of $1,400

2. a 12% commission rate on a sale of $22,500

3. a 9% commission rate on a sale of $13,400

4. a 25% commission rate on a sale of $58,200

APPLICATIONS

5. Boyd is an insurance agent for a company that pays a commission of 40% of the first year's premium. What will Boyd's commission be if he sells a life insurance policy with a first year premium of $1,180.

6. Anna is the owner of Second-Hand Kids, a children's consignment shop. Anna receives a commission of 25% of all sales. How much did Anna make if sales this month totaled $4,900?

7. Peter is a salesman for a car dealership. He makes a 4% commission on his total sales for the month. This month Peter had a total of $144,000 in car sales. How much commission did Peter earn this month?

8. Norma works for an art gallery. She receives an 8% commission on each painting she sells. This week Norma sold paintings which cost $950, $480, $1,260, and $390. How much commission did she earn this week?

9. Randy is a salesman for a furniture store. He receives a salary of $15,000 per year plus a commission of 12% of his total annual sales. During one year, Randy had a total of $135,000 in sales. How much commission did Randy make that year? What were Randy's total earnings for the year?

10. Marsha is a door-to-door salesperson for a vacuum cleaner company. She receives a salary of $150 per week plus a commission of 16% on all sales over $1,000. How much money did Marsha earn during a week when her sales totaled $2,700?

Check your answers on page 109.

LESSON 8   Percent of Increase

Words to KNOW

The **percent of increase** is an expression of a ratio of the difference between two values and the original value. If gasoline used to cost $1.00 per gallon, and its price rises to $1.05 per gallon, then an increase of $ .05 has taken place. In this case, $.05 is called the **amount of increase**. The **original value** is the price the gasoline used to be before the increase. Dividing the amount of increase by the original value provides a decimal which, when converted, becomes the percent of increase.

Kathy is a secretary for an insurance company. Over the last year Kathy has increased her typing speed from 60 words per minute to 75 words per minute.

Percent of increase is used to show how much a quantity has increased over its original value.

Percent of increase

To find a percent of increase, subtract the new value from the original value, and then divide this difference by the original value.

Kathy's supervisor wants her to determine the percent of increase in her typing speed. To determine this increase, Kathy will follow the steps below.

EXAMPLE 1

Find the percent of increase in typing speed from 60 words per minute to 75 words per minute.

Step 1   Subtract the **original value** (60) from the new value (75). The difference (15) is the **amount of increase**.

$$75 - 60 = 15$$

Step 2   Divide the amount of increase by the original value: $15 \div 60 = .25$.

$$
\begin{array}{r}
.25 \\
60\overline{)15.00} \\
-120 \\
\hline
300 \\
-300 \\
\hline
0
\end{array}
$$

Step 3   Change the decimal to a percent.

$$.25 = 25\%$$

EXERCISE 8

Find the percent of increase.

1. an increase from 50 words per minute to 80 words per minute

2. an increase from $8 an hour to $11 an hour

3. an increase from 1,500 employees to 2,100 employees

4. an increase from $6 an hour to $9 an hour

APPLICATION

5. When Kathy was hired she received $10 an hour. She just received a raise and now earns $10.50 an hour. What percent of increase in pay did Kathy receive?

Check your answers on page 109.

When finding percent of increase, subtract the original amount from the new amount. Then divide this number by the original amount.

USE WHAT YOU HAVE LEARNED

Find the percent of increase.

1. an increase from 50 words per minute to 65 words per minute

2. an increase from 20 employees to 32 employees

3. an increase from $12 an hour to $15 an hour

4. an increase from $40,000 a year to $42,000 a year

APPLICATIONS

5. The insurance company that Kathy works for has increased its number of employees from 50 to 70. What is the percent of increase in the number of employees?

6. Arnold is a bartender who makes $6.50 an hour, plus tips. He received a raise and now makes $7.41 an hour. What is Arnold's percent of increase in his hourly pay?

7. Arnold, the bartender, normally works 24 hours a week. His boss is now scheduling him to work 33 hours a week? What percent of increase is this?

8. Patrice is the assistant manager of a landscaping company. She is figuring the percent of increase in sales for the first two quarters of this year. Sales during the first quarter of the year totaled $25,500. Sales during the second quarter totaled $43,860. What is the percent of increase in sales?

9. Gil works for a construction company making $324 a week. Gil just received a raise and now makes $351.54 a week. What is Gil's amount of increase? What is his percent of increase?

10. Linda is a teacher's aide who made $18,800 last year. This year she is making $20,492. What is Linda's amount of salary increase? What is her percent of increase?

Check your answers on page 110.

LESSON 9   Percent of Decrease

Words to KNOW

The **percent of decrease** is an expression of a ratio of the difference between two values and an original value. If gasoline used to cost $1.00 per gallon, and its price drops to $0.95 per gallon, then a decrease of $ .05 has taken place. In this case, $.05 is called the **amount of decrease.** The **original value** is the price the gasoline used to be before the decrease. Dividing the amount of decrease by the original value provides a decimal which, when converted, becomes the percent of decrease.

Blake owns a small gift shop. He is looking over his electricity bills for the past 2 months.

Percent of decrease

Percent of decrease is used to show how much a quantity has decreased from its original value. The procedure to figure percent of decrease is similar to the procedure used to figure percent of increase.

Blake notices that last month his electric bill was $60. This month it is $52.80. To determine the percent of decrease in his electric bill, Blake follows the steps below.

EXAMPLE 1

Find the percent of decrease in electric bills of $60 and $52.80.

Step 1 Subtract the new value from the **original value**: $60 - 52.8 = 7.20$. This amount (7.20) is called the **amount of decrease.**

$$\begin{array}{r} 60.00 \\ -52.80 \\ \hline 7.20 \end{array}$$

Step 2 Divide the amount of decrease by the original value: $7.20 \div 60 = .12$. (This step is exactly the same as that used to find percent of increase.)

$$\begin{array}{r} .12 \\ 60\overline{)7.20} \\ -\underline{60} \\ 120 \\ -\underline{120} \\ 0 \end{array}$$

Step 3 Change the decimal to a percent.

$.12 = 12\%$

EXERCISE 9

Find the percent of decrease.

1. a decrease from 3.5 minutes to 2.8 minutes

2. a decrease from $8 an hour to $7.44 an hour

3. a decrease from 120 employees to 99 employees

4. a decrease from 72 degrees to 54 degrees

APPLICATION

5. Blake, the gift shop owner, had 8 employees during the holiday season. He has now cut back to only 5 employees. What percent of decrease does this represent?

Check your answers on page 110.

When finding percent of decrease, subtract the new amount from the original amount. Then divide this number by the original amount.

USE WHAT YOU HAVE LEARNED

Find the percent of decrease.

1. a decrease from a $50 bonus to a $40 bonus

2. a decrease from 250 employees to 225 employees

3. a decrease from $12 an hour to $10.50 an hour

4. a decrease from $32,500 a year to $28,925 a year

APPLICATIONS

5. Blake's gift shop had sales of $16,400 during December. In January the sales dropped to $8,528. What percent of decrease does this represent?

6. Kayla is the bookkeeper for a small retail store. A new computer was purchased which reduced the time it takes for Kayla to print the payroll checks. It used to take 25 minutes, and now it takes only 15 minutes. What percent of decrease does this represent?

7. Marie works for a preschool. She is looking over the enrollment records. Last year, the total enrollment was 60 children. This year, the enrollment is 51 children. What percent of decrease does this represent?

8. Karen runs an arts and crafts store. Karen wants to reduce her electric bill, so she turns her heating thermostat down from 75 degrees to 69 degrees. What percent of decrease does this represent?

9. Trevor is the manager of a small appliance store. Due to a decrease in demand for blenders, Trevor reduced the orders for these from 20 per month to 8 per month. What percent of decrease does this represent?

10. Trevor's small appliance store has a sale in progress. Microwave ovens that usually cost $280 each have been reduced to $196 each. What percent of decrease does this represent?

Check your answers on page 111.

LESSON 10   Pie Graphs and Bar Graphs

Clarence is an assembly worker for the Motown Motor Company. The Motown Factory produced 345,000 cars last year. There are four production shifts. The production figures for the preceding year came out in the company newsletter, and Clarence wanted to know how his shift measured up against the other production shifts.

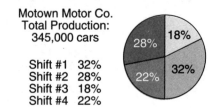

Motown Motor Co.
Total Production:
345,000 cars

Shift #1   32%
Shift #2   28%
Shift #3   18%
Shift #4   22%

Pie graphs

Pie (or circle) graphs are used to show the relationship of various parts to the whole. The entire graph represents 100%. The parts are shown as percents.

EXAMPLE 1

Find the number of cars produced by Shift #1.

Step 1	Find the whole. Identify the total number of cars produced from the information on the chart.	**345,000** cars
Step 2	Find the percent. Identify the percent of cars produced by Shift #1 from the chart.	32%
Step 3	Convert the percent to a decimal.	**32%** = .32
Step 4	Multiply the total number of cars produced (the whole) by the decimal.	345,000 ×.32 690000 +10350000 110,400.00 cars

EXERCISE 10A

APPLICATIONS

1. How many cars did Shift #2 produce?

2. How many more cars were produced by Shift #1 than Shift #2?

3. What was the total number of cars produced by Shifts #3 and #4 ?

4. How many more cars will Shift #4 have to produce to equal Shift #1's production?

5. Did the first two shifts or the last two shifts produce more cars for Motown?

Check your answers on page 111.

Bar Graphs

Another common form of graphic representation is the bar graph. Bar graphs can also be used to show the relationship of the whole to its parts. Information on bar graphs can be used to calculate percents.

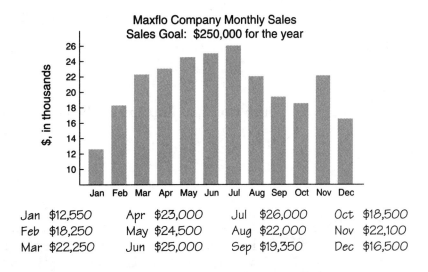

Jan $12,550	Apr $23,000	Jul $26,000	Oct $18,500
Feb $18,250	May $24,500	Aug $22,000	Nov $22,100
Mar $22,250	Jun $25,000	Sep $19,350	Dec $16,500

The Maxflo Company's sales goal for the year is $250,000. This bar graph shows the Maxflo Company's sales in each month.

EXAMPLE 2

What percent of the annual goal did Maxflo sell in March?

Step 1	Find the whole. Identify the annual sales goal from the information on the graph.	$250,000
Step 2	Find the part. Identify the sales in the month of March.	$22,250
Step 3	Divide the sales in March by the annual sales goal.	$\dfrac{\$22{,}250}{\$250{,}000} = .089$
Step 4	Convert the decimal to a percent.	$.08.9 = 8.9\%$

EXERCISE 10B

Calculate the percent of Maxflo's sales goal each month's sales represents. Round to the nearest whole percent.

6. Jan	9. Apr	12. Jul	15. Oct
7. Feb	10. May	13. Aug	16. Nov
8. Mar	11. Jun	14. Sep	17. Dec

APPLICATION

18. Which month at Maxflo had the lowest sales?

Check your answers on page 112.

Examine all of the information on a graph before you attempt to use it. Look at the title and captions, note how the sides of the graph are labeled, and read any instructions or other data that accompany the graph. Do not try to use a graph until you fully understand what it represents.

USE WHAT YOU HAVE LEARNED

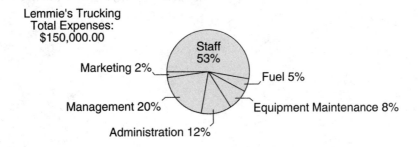

Lemmie's Trucking
Total Expenses:
$150,000.00

Staff 53%

Marketing 2%

Fuel 5%

Management 20%

Equipment Maintenance 8%

Administration 12%

Answer the following questions based on information in the graph above.

1. How much does Lemmie's Trucking Company spend on administration?

2. What percent of the company's expenses are for equipment repairs and maintenance?

3. How much does this company spend on fuel?

4. What percent of this company's expenses go for marketing?

The following questions refer back to the three graphs previously introduced in the lesson.

APPLICATIONS

5. Since Lemmie's Trucking company has only one manager, how much does he earn?

6. What percent of the annual expenses of Lemmie's Trucking company were spent on salaries and wages?

7. How much money was spent on fuel and equipment maintenance?

8. Each shift at Motown Factory has 1,000 workers. Any shift producing 95,000 or more cars receives a bonus of $100 per person. How much money did this company pay out in bonuses?

9. The shift with the lowest production also had the highest rate of absenteeism, 7.9%. If there were 260 work days, how many days were missed by workers on this shift?

10. Which quarter, Jan.-Mar, Apr - Jun, Jul-Sep, Oct-Dec, had the highest sales foe Maxflo Co?

11. Did Maxflo's lowest sales month occur in the lowest sales quarter? Did the highest sales month occur in the highest sales quarter?

Check your answers on page 112.

LESSON 11 Using Information from Graphs

Michelle, secretary to the president of Custom Commuter Service, is examining a report. The Custom Commuter Service Airlines Reservations Department presented the table below to show its growth.

Custom Commuter Service Airlines
Commuter Trips/year – Austin San Antonio

1991 ✈ ✈ ✈ ✈ ✈ ✈

1992 ✈ ✈ ✈ ✈ ✈

1993 ✈ ✈ ✈ ✈ ✈ ✈ ✈

1994 ✈ ✈ ✈ ✈ ✈ ✈ ✈ ✈

1995 ✈ ✈ ✈ ✈ ✈ ✈ ✈ ✈ ✈ ✈

Each plane represents 100 commuter trips between Austin and San Antonio.

Using Information from Simple Graphs

Graphs are pictorial representations of information. It is up to the reader to select and process the information. Here, you see the steps Michelle used to convert the information on the graph into information she could use to compute the percent of increase.

EXAMPLE 1

What is the percent of increase in flights between 1994 and 1995?

Step 1 Survey all of the information about the graph. Read the title, the labels of columns and rows, and information about the meanings of the symbols used.

Title: Computer trips/year
Labels: rows labeled by year, 1991-95
Symbols: each plane equals 100 flights

Step 2 Examine the problem closely. Decide precisely what information from the graph is necessary to answer the particular problem.

Determine the total number of flights in 1994 and 1995. Find the total number of flights recorded in the rows labeled 1994 and 1995.

Step 3 Count the number of plane symbols in rows 1994 (8) and 1995 (10) and multiply each total by 100. Find the percent of increase.

$8 \times 100 = 800$
$10 \times 100 = 1,000$

$\frac{1000 - 800}{800} = \frac{200}{800} = 25 = 25\%$

Take a few moments to becomes as familiar as you can with a graph before trying to use it. Pay special attention to the labels on the graph. Make sure you understand what they mean.

EXERCISE 11A

Use the graph on page 47 to answer the following questions.

APPLICATIONS

1. Which year experienced a decrease in flights from the preceding year?

2. Flights in 1992 were what percent of flights in 1993?

3. Which year experienced the largest percent of increase over the preceding year?

Check your answers on page 112.

Using Information from Complex Graphs

The bar graph at right shows hypothetical federal spending in three areas, Health, Education, and Welfare (HEW), Environmental Protection (EP), and Economic Development (DEV) for the years 1991-1995 in the fictitious country of Americus. Fred, a financial analyst, has to find out what the percent of increase in spending for Health Education and Welfare occurred from 1992 to 1993.

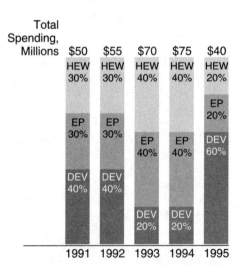

EXAMPLE 2

What is the percent of increase in spending for HEW from 1992 to 1993.

Step 1 Read the question carefully and determine just what is being asked.

Step 2 Review the graph to select the piece of information which is most relevant to the question.

HEW = 30% of $55,000,000 in 1992
HEW = 40% of $70,000,000 in 1993

Step 3 Perform any operations necessary to determine the answer

HEW = 30% of $55,000,000 in 1992
HEW = .3 × $55,000,000
HEW = $16,500,000 in 1992
HEW = 40% of $70,000,000 in 1993
HEW = .4 × $70,000,000
HEW = 28,000,000 in 1993

$$\text{Percent of increase} = \frac{\text{new amount} - \text{old amount}}{\text{old amount}}$$

$$\text{Percent of increase} = \frac{28,000,000 - 16,500,000}{16,500,000}$$

$$\text{Percent of increase} = \frac{11,500,000}{16,500,000} = \frac{115}{165} = .70 = 70\%$$

EXERCISE 11B

Using the graph on the page 48, answer the following questions.

APPLICATIONS

4. Was there an increase or a decrease in spending between 1991 and 1995?

5. How much money was spent in 1994 on environmental protection?

6. What is the total increase in spending between 1991 and 1993?

7. What was the percent of increase in spending on economic development between 1994 and 1995?

Check your answers
on page 113.

8. In which years, if any, did the percent spending in environmental protection remain the same?

USE WHAT YOU HAVE LEARNED

Use the graph on page 48 to answer the following questions.

APPLICATIONS

1. Calculate the percent of decrease in spending in HEW between 1994 and 1995. If the Department must lay off the same percent of workers and there are 45,550 employees, how many jobs would be cut?

2. Ned, who works for a newspaper, is collecting background information for an article about the environment. What was the percent of increase or decrease in spending on Environmental Protection between 1992 and 1993?

3. What was the average amount in dollars spent in Health, Education and Welfare during the five year period shown on the graph?

4. Mary, a secretary at the Chamber of Commerce, is double checking facts in a report for her boss. Was more money spent on economic development in 1994 or 1995?

Check your answers
on page 113.

CHAPTER 2 Summary

In this chapter you learned to compute commission, the percent of increase, and the percent of decrease. You also learned techniques for using information from graphs.

Finding Commissions

To find the amount of a commission, change the percent to a decimal, and multiply the percent by the total of the sales.

EXERCISE A

Check your answers on page 114.

Find the commission.

1. A 15% commission rate on a sale of $1,880

2. A 12% commission rate on a sale of $11,300

3. A 6% commission rate on a sale of $72,360

4. A 20% commission rate on a sale of $835

Percent of Increase

To find percent of increase, subtract the original value from the new value. This amount is called the amount of increase. Divide the amount of increase by the original value, and then change the decimal to a percent.

EXERCISE B

Check your answers on page 114.

Find the percent of increase.

5. An increase from 40 words per minute to 65 words per minute

6. An increase from $6 an hour to $8 an hour

7. An increase from 1,200 employees to 2,200 employees

8. An increase from $20,000 per year to $26,000 per year

Percent of Decrease

To find percent of decrease, subtract the new value from the original value. This amount is called the amount of decrease. Divide the amount of decrease by the original value, and then change the decimal to a percent.

EXERCISE C

Find the percent of decrease.

9. A decrease from a $36 phone bill to a $27 phone bill

10. A decrease from 150 employees to 125 employees

11. A decrease from $10 an hour to $9.50 an hour

12. A decrease from $32,000 per year to $22,000 per year

Check your answers on page 114.

Pie Graphs

Pie (or circle) graphs are often used to show the relationship of various parts to the whole. The entire graph represents 100%. The parts are shown as percents.

EXERCISE D

The graph at right represents the payroll of the Glower Company for the last year. Fifteen percent of all employee payroll was paid into Social Security, 12% to income tax, and 10% to the company sponsored insurance plan. The rest of the graph represents the employees' take-home pay.

Glower Company
Annual Payroll: $464,000

Social Security 15%

Insurance 10%

Income Tax 12%

Take-home Pay

13. What percent of the payroll is represented by take-home pay?

14. How many dollars were paid for Social Security last year?

Check your answers on page 114.

15. How many dollars were paid in Social Security and Income Tax?

MATH AT WORK

1. **Insurance Agent**   John and Boyd, insurance agents, work for a 30% commission on the first $80,000 they sell. If their sales are more than $80,000, they receive 40% on the whole amount. John sold $78,550 and Boyd sold $82,500. What were their annual commissions?

2. **Landscaper**   Leonardo's Lawn Lovers maintenance company has increased the number of employees from 23 to 33 in the last year? What is the percent increase in the number of employees?

3. **Baker**   Penny's pastries had record sales of $35,000 in December but returned to normal in January with $27,500. What was the percent decrease in sales?

4. **Retail Clerk**   Last month Anna earned a 25% commission on $4,900. This month she sold $5,300. How much did she earn in the last two months?

5. **Server**   Ella received a raise in pay from $6.25 per hour to $7.00 per hour. What was her percent increase in pay?

6. **Line Worker**   New machinery on the assembly line has enabled Joe to assemble one unit in 4 minutes and 15 seconds instead of 6 minutes and 30 sec. What is the percent decrease in time?

7. **Automobile Salesperson**   Pete earned 4% on $154,000 of auto sales last month. This month he made the Manager's Circle by selling $210,500. This earned him a commission of 5%. What was his commission this month?

8. **Maintenance Worker**   Last month Arnold earned $\frac{\$6.50}{hr}$ and worked 24 hours. This month he got a raise to $\frac{\$7.00}{hr}$ and worked 30 hours. How much more did he earn? What was the percent of increase in his pay?

9. **Counselor**   The number of absentee days at Edgewater Middle School last year was 4,035. This year, since Mr. H. Jones was hired as a counselor/truant officer, there were only 3,123. What was the percent of decrease in absentee days since Mr. Jones was hired?

10. **Art Dealer**   Norma earned 8% commission on two paintings which sold for $950 and $1,250 and 10% commission on two sculptures which sold for $2,250 and $4,500. What was her total commission?

11. **Sales Manager**   A pie graph shows 28% of the total income of a company is due to referrals and 35% of the total income is due to advertising. The balance of income is due to telemarketing. If the company's total income is $110,000, how much is due to telemarketing?

12. **Real Estate Agent**   Randy, a real estate agent, earns a base salary of $15,000 a year plus a commission of 2% on his annual sales. If he sells a total of $1,650,000 what is his average monthly salary?

13. **Newspaper Publisher** The New Age News has increased its circulation from 10,245 to 12,550 in three months. What is the percent of increase?

14. **Retail Manager** Great Buys discount store sells food processors for $129.95, which is a $30 savings of the regular price. A regular department store sells 28 food processors per month at the regular price and Great Buys sells 56. Food processor sales at Great Buys is what percent of food processor sales at the regular department store?

15. **Vacuum Cleaner Salesperson** Marta sells dust mite vacuum cleaners, door to door. She increased her sales calls from 25 to 56 and her sales increased from $2,700 to $3,650. Did her percent increase of sales calls equal the percent increase in her sales?

16. **Real Estate Agent** Jack has been working on a big real estate deal for six months. He is successful at selling a piece of land for $1.3 million at 10% commission. His office mate Frank has sold 7 housing development lots for $95,000 at 12% commission in the same six months. Who made more money? How much more?

17. **Real Estate Agent** In problem number 16, Jack's commission was what percent greater than Frank's commission?

18. **Secretary** The secretary in Mel's office gets a commission for service contracts she sells over the phone. So far this month she has sold 14 preventative maintenance contracts for $90 each at 7% and 12 full service contracts for $180 each at 8%. How much commission has she earned so far?

19. **Marketer** This circle graph shows the earnings of ABCD Music Company in terms of rock, country, classical, and alternative music. If total sales were $245,000, what was the difference between the total sales of country music and alternative music?

ABCD Music Co.
Total Sales: $245,000

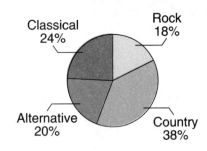

Classical 24%
Rock 18%
Alternative 20%
Country 38%

20. **Retail Salesperson** Anne buys health care products worth $1,265. She marks them up by 25% for sale. How much profit does she make once she has sold all the products?

21. **Retail Salesperson** If Anne sells $1,555 worth of health care products at 25% and $750 worth of a new product at 42% commission, how much will she earn?

22. **Automobile Salesperson** At Quality Used Cars Dealership, foreign-made car sales decreased from 5,255 to 4,355 in one year. Sales of domestic cars increased from 3,490 to 5,655. What was the percent of decrease in foreign-made cars and the percent of increase in domestic cars?

23. **Retail Salesperson** Alex is selling home cleaning products part time to supplement his regular salary of $1,800 per month. If he sells $1,245 at 30% commission, how much will he earn this month?

Check your answers on page 115.

CHAPTER 3

The Part, the Whole, the Percent

LESSON 12   Finding Part of a Number

Sonya sells cellular phones. She earns a 15% commission on her sales. This month Sonya sells $1,450 worth of phones and equipment. Sonya renames the percent as a decimal amount and then multiplies it by the total amount of her sales to find how much commission she will make.

$$15\% = .15$$

$$
\begin{array}{r}
\$1450 \\
\times\ .15 \\
\hline
7250 \\
14500 \\
\hline
\$217.50
\end{array}
$$

The illustration above shows how Sonya calculates the amount of her commission. Sonya's commission is a part of the whole amount represented by her total sales.

Finding the Part Based on the Percent and the Whole

A **part** of an amount is found by multiplying the whole amount by the decimal form of the percent. The whole times the percent equals the part.

Sonya earns a 3% bonus each quarter when her sales top $6,000. She sold $7,290 this quarter. How much is Sonya's bonus?

EXAMPLE 1

Find 3% of 7,290.

Step 1	Rename 3% as the decimal .03.	$3\% = .03$
Step 2	Multiply the whole by the decimal form of the percent.	$\begin{array}{r}\$7,290 \\ \times\ .03 \\ \hline 21870 \\ +00000 \\ \hline \$218.70\end{array}$

EXERCISE 12

Find the parts in the following problems.

   1. 19% of 45 =

   2. 5% of 178 =

   3. 125% of $51 =

   4. 33% of $296.99 =

   5. 40% of 95 =

   6. 37.5 % of 169 =

   7. 75% of $47.25 =

   8. 20% of $172 =

APPLICATION

Check your answers
on page 117.

9. The music store Joan works in is having a sale. All CDs are 20% off. If a CD costs $12.99, how much will a customer save?

MATH TIP

When finding part of a number, you can use either decimals or fractions. Find the method that is quicker and easier for you.

USE WHAT YOU HAVE LEARNED

Find the part in each of the following problems.

   1. 12% of 50 =

   2. 117% of 286 =

   3. 65% of 50 =

   4. 18% of 1,880 =

   5. 15% of 75 =

   6. 136% of 121 =

   7. 25% of 50

   8. 0.3% of 86

9. Mark manages 30 employees. 80% of them are full time. How many full time employees does Mark manage?

10. Sandy has 30 children at her daycare center. 30% of them are 2 years old or younger. How many of the children are 2 or younger?

11. During the month of June, Tom is selling all televisions at 15% off. A customer wants to buy a television that is $895.99. How much will the customer save?

12. Paul owns an insurance company. He has 8 employees. He wants to increase the number of employees by 125% within five years. How many people will Paul need to hire to reach his goal? How many employees will work for Paul if he reaches his goal?

13. In an informal music survey for a rock radio station, Ginger found that 62.5% of the 408 listeners were between the ages of 17 and 29. How many of the listeners were not between the ages of 17 and 29?

14. The clothes store is having a 25%-off sale on the purchase of any item in the store. Susan sells a blouse that costs $28. How much will the customer save? How much will the blouse cost? If the tax rate is 7.5%, what will be the total cost the customer will pay?

15. Isako earns $578.93 each week. If she saves 5% each week, how much does she save? How much will Isako save in a year?

Check your answers on page 118.

LESSON 13   Finding a Number from its Percent

Donald books tours for a travel agency. 54 people have signed up for a trip to Las Vegas. The tour is 75% full. Donald wants to find the total number of people who can take the trip. Donald converts the percent into a decimal. Then he divides to find how many people can go to Las Vegas.

$$75\% = .75$$

$$
\begin{array}{r}
72. \\
75.\overline{)5400.} \\
525 \\
\hline
150 \\
150 \\
\hline
0
\end{array}
$$

The problem above shows how Donald finds the number of people he can sign up for the tour. The 54 people already signed up for the tour are a part of a whole. The percent represents that part.

Finding the Whole From the Percent and the Part

To find the **whole** if given the percent and a part, divide the part by the decimal form of the percent.

Donald booked 232 trips for customers last month. He provided 40% of the company's business. How many trips did the company arrange for the month?

EXAMPLE 1

232 ÷ 40% = ?

Step 1   Rewrite 40% as the decimal .4.   *40% = .40 or .4*

Step 2   Divide the known part by the decimal form of the percent.

$$
\begin{array}{r}
580. \\
4.\overline{)2,320.} \\
-20 \\
\hline
32 \\
-32 \\
\hline
00
\end{array}
$$

EXERCISE 13

Find the wholes.

1. 19 is 25% of ?

2. 687 is 79% of ?

3. $42.68 is 2% of ?

4. 345 is 16% of ?

APPLICATION

5. Uki has processed 438 semi-conductor wafers. That is 60% of the order. How many wafers were in the order?

Check your answers on page 119.

If you feel more comfortable dividing by fractions instead of decimals, rename the percent as a fraction. Then divide.

USE WHAT YOU HAVE LEARNED

Find the wholes.

1. 42 is 15% of ?

2. 56 is 70% of ?

3. 501 is 80% of ?

4. 63 is 35% of ?

5. 28 is 10% of ?

6. 9.84 is 3% of ?

7. $7.56 is 21% of ?

8. $926.72 is 64% of ?

APPLICATIONS

9. Marie spends 40% of her work day delivering mail to people within the company. She delivers mail for 3 hours each day. How many hours does Marie work each day?

10. John is a car salesman. There are 72 trucks on the lot. That is 45% of the inventory. How many vehicles are on the car lot?

11. Rodney is to help deliver a shipment of food to a grocery store. 117 boxes fit in his truck. The boxes are only 25% of what the store is to receive. How many boxes are to be delivered to the store?

12. Marco is making a draw on a customer's interim financing loan for a house he is building. He has completed 33% of the house. With this draw, Marco will have used $28,710 of the original loan. What was the original size of the account?

13. Zack bought 4 100-foot strings of Christmas lights to hang around the roof of his restaurant's patio. He found that the 4 strings only covered 80% of the distance he wanted to decorate. How many feet of lights does Zack need in order to finish? How many more strings of lights like those already purchased will he need?

14. A department store is having a 50% off sale on gold rings. Louisa sells 108, or 90%, of the rings within the first four hours. If Louisa is selling the rings for $89.50, what is the original price? How many rings did the store have in stock for the sale?

Check your answers on page 119.

LESSON 14 Finding the Original Price

Tara operates a bed and breakfast. She bought a bedspread for $46.80 after it had been reduced 20%. To find how much the bedspread originally cost, Tara subtracts the percent of savings from 100%. She converts the difference into a decimal. Then she divides the decimal into the amount she paid to find the original selling price.

$$
\begin{array}{r}
100\% \\
-\ 20\% \\
\hline
80\%
\end{array}
\qquad
80\% = .8
\qquad
\begin{array}{r}
\$58.50 \\
8.\overline{)\$468.00} \\
\underline{40} \\
68 \\
\underline{64} \\
40 \\
\underline{40} \\
00
\end{array}
$$

The problem above shows how Tara finds the original price of a sale item. The sale price of the bedspread is a part of the whole.

Using Percent to Find the Original Price

To find the original price, or whole amount, first find the difference between 100% and the percent of the discount. Then divide the price paid by the decimal form of the percent difference.

Tara charges repeat customers $63 to stay at her bed and breakfast. It is a 10% savings off the original price. What do first time visitors pay to stay at Tara's bed and breakfast?

EXAMPLE 1

Percent of discount = 10%   Sale price = $63   What is the original price?

Step 1 Subtract the discount percent from 100% to find the difference.

$$
\begin{array}{r}
100\% \\
-\ 10\% \\
\hline
90\%
\end{array}
$$

Step 2 Convert 90% to the decimal .90.

$$90\% = .90$$

Step 3 Divide the price paid by the decimal form of the percent difference.

$$
\begin{array}{r}
\$70. \\
90.\overline{)\$6,300.} \\
\underline{-\ 630} \\
00
\end{array}
$$

EXERCISE 14

Find the original price.

1. Discount 20%
   Sale price $16

2. Discount 70%
   Sale price $4.50

3. Discount 25%
   Sale price $45

4. Discount 75%
   Sale price $206

APPLICATION

5. Nina is marking down a rack of winter clothes by 40%. If a sweater costs $24.33 now, what was the original price?

Check your answers on page 120.

If you feel more comfortable dividing by fractions instead of decimals, rename the percent as a fraction. Then divide.

USE WHAT YOU HAVE LEARNED

Find the original price.

1. Discount 5%
   Sale price $3.80

2. Discount 30%
   Sale price $98

3. Discount 75%
   Sale price $42

4. Discount 20%
   Sale price $260

5. Discount 67%
   Sale price $99

6. Discount 40%
   Sale price $19.50

7. Discount 20%
   Sale price $58

8. Discount 34%
   Sale price $13.20

APPLICATIONS

9. Doug has a 25% discount coupon. He pays $525 for a fax machine. What was the original price of the fax machine?

10. Eric can lease an office for $729 per month for one year and get a 20% discount. After one year, the original price will take effect. What will Eric pay after the one year is up?

11. Marilyn buys a brief case for $52.80. It was 34% off. What was the original price of the brief case?

12. Ann owns a tack and feed store. She buys a saddle at a wholesale price of $297. It is 50% off the retail price. What is the retail price of the saddle?

13. Fran is buying shirts for the company baseball team. She can get 15 shirts for $5.70 each with a 5% discount. If she buys 20 shirts, she will get 10% off the original price of each shirt. What is the original cost of each shirt? What is the cost of each shirt if Fran orders 20 shirts? How much can Fran save per shirt if she orders 20 shirts?

14. Sandra caters dinners for businesses and parties. One business has ordered 120 steak dinners for a banquet. She gives the company a 15% discount and contracts to supply the dinners for $7.99 a plate. What does Sandra usually charge for a steak dinner? What will be the savings to the company off the total amount?

Check your answers on page 120.

LESSON 15   Finding Percent from Part and Whole

The county extension agent asks Rob what percent of his land he uses for dairy cattle. Rob has 85 acres of land. He uses 34 acres to raise dairy cows. He uses his remaining land to raise crops. Rob divides the 34 acres used for dairy cows by the whole 85 acres. Then he coverts the decimal to a percent.

$$85\overline{)34.00} \quad \underline{.40} \qquad .40 = 40\%$$

$$\underline{340}$$
$$00$$

The problem above shows how Rob finds the percent of land used for raising the dairy cattle. He divides the part by the whole amount. This is the procedure you will use to find what percent one number is of the whole amount.

Finding the Percent

To find what percent a part of a number is of the whole, divide the part by the whole amount. Rename the decimal in the quotient as a percent.

Of the 51 acres that Rob has for crops, 17 are used for feed corn. What percent of the crop land is used for corn?

EXAMPLE 1

17 is ? percent of 51

Step 1   Set up the division problem so that the part is divided by the whole. Work the problem.

Step 2   Rename the decimal as a percent.

$$51\overline{)17.00} \quad \underline{.33}$$
$$\underline{-153}$$
$$170$$
$$\underline{-153}$$
$$17$$

$$33\%$$

EXERCISE 15

Find the percent.

1. 9 is ? percent of 36

2. 26 is ? percent of 65

3. 12 is ? percent of 96

APPLICATION

4. Ginger has unpacked 13 of 100 boxes of jeans. What is the percent of boxes she has unpacked?

Check your answers
on page 121.

To find what percent an unknown part is of the whole, subtract the known part from the whole. Then divide the difference by the whole amount. Rename the decimal in the quotient as a percent.

USE WHAT YOU HAVE LEARNED

Find the percent.

1. .09 is ? percent of 9

2. 12 is ? percent of 18

3. 54 is ? percent of 900

4. 4 is ? percent of 10

5. 56 is ? percent of 80

6. 48 is ? percent of 64

7. Molly's company has 125 employees. They are encouraging everyone to donate blood. So far, 85 employees have done so. What percent of employees donated blood?

8. Juan works in a book store. A $4.80 book is on sale for $3.00. What percent was the book reduced?

9. Monica manages a day care center with 72 children. There are two classes of four-year-olds that have 9 children each. What percent of the children at day care are four years old?

10. Ada buys a television that costs $980. After paying the deposit, she has $852 left to pay. What percent deposit did she make? If Ada makes 6 equal payments, how much will she pay each month?

11. Pete pays $68 per night for a room that normally costs $80. He is able to get the reduced rate because of his frequent traveler discount card. He also uses the discount card to pay for a dinner that normally costs $23.40. How much discount does Pete get with the card? What will be the price of his dinner with the card?

12. Don is a district manager of a toy store. He is to drive a total of 1,550 miles to visit 9 stores. He has been to 2 stores and gone 403 miles. What percent of stores has he visited? What percent of miles does he have left to drive?

Check your answers on page 122.

LESSON 16 Applying Proportion to Percent Problems

Jamal needs to order concrete to finish a slab he is pouring. 80% of the slab is finished. So far, he has used 48 cubic yards of concrete. Jamal realizes that the 48 cubic yards already used represents a part of the whole amount needed to finish the job. He also has the percent of the floor already completed. He knows he can compute the whole and subtract 48 from it to get a figure for the remaining concrete, but can't remember whether to multiply or divide the part and the percent.

The Proportional Method to Solve Percent Problems

In Lesson 1, percent was defined as a way of expressing "how many out of one hundred." Percent can be expressed as a fraction with a denominator of 100.

$$42\% = \frac{42}{100}$$

Any percent problem can be expressed as a proportion. Simply create a fraction with the part as numerator and the whole as denominator. Use the percent as the numerator of the second fraction, with 100 as the denominator. Once the problem is set up, "cross-multiply and divide."

$$\frac{part}{whole} = \frac{\%}{100}$$

Jamal can't remember whether to multiply or divide, so he creates a proportion.

EXAMPLE 1

48 is 80% of ?

Step 1 First, Jamal sets out the proportion: part over whole equals percent over 100.

$$\frac{part}{whole} = \frac{\%}{100}$$

Step 2 Jamal substitutes the values from his problem into his proportion. The number 48 replaces the word "part." The percent is written as a whole number (not a decimal) above the 100. The question is asking for the whole, so the denominator under the 48 (part) is not known.

$$\frac{48}{?} = \frac{80}{100}$$

Step 3 Since you're working with fractions, reduce. $\frac{80}{100}$ reduces to $\frac{4}{5}$.

$$\frac{48}{?} = \frac{4}{5} \frac{80}{100}$$

Step 4 Cross multiply. Look at the diagonal pairs indicated by the lines. 48 and 5 are a cross-pair. 4 and ? are a cross-pair. Multiply whichever pair contains two numbers: in this case, $48 \times 5 = 240$.

$$\require{cancel}\frac{48}{?} = \frac{4}{5} \quad 240$$

$$\frac{48}{?} = \frac{4}{5} \qquad \begin{array}{r} 60 \\ 4\overline{)240} \\ -24 \\ \hline 00 \end{array}$$

Step 5 Divide the product, 240, by the remaining number, 4. $240 \div 4 = 60$. This quotient is the missing number, in this case, the whole.

$$\frac{48}{60} = \frac{80}{100}$$

The whole job requires 60 cubic yards of cement. Jamal has already poured 48 cubic yards. He needs to order $60 - 48$ or 12 yards to complete the job.

EXERCISE 16

Cross multiply and divide to find the missing value. Reduce the fractions to make your work easier whenever possible.

1. $\dfrac{5}{?} = \dfrac{20}{100}$

2. $\dfrac{48}{64} = \dfrac{?}{100}$

3. $\dfrac{?}{588} = \dfrac{68}{100}$

4. $\dfrac{45}{?} = \dfrac{40}{100}$

5. $\dfrac{450}{250} = \dfrac{?}{100}$

6. $\dfrac{?}{348} = \dfrac{88}{100}$

APPLICATION

7. Mara is traveling to a seminar in Philadelphia. She has driven 652 miles. She is 60% of the way there. What is the total number of miles Mara will travel to get to Philadelphia? Use a proportion to solve.

Check your answers on page 122.

USE WHAT YOU HAVE LEARNED

Cross multiply and divide to find the missing value. Reduce the fractions to make your work easier whenever possible.

1. $\dfrac{44}{?} = \dfrac{25}{100}$

2. $\dfrac{64}{80} = \dfrac{?}{100}$

3. $\dfrac{?}{600} = \dfrac{40}{100}$

4. $\dfrac{38}{?} = \dfrac{19}{100}$

5. $\dfrac{225}{125} = \dfrac{?}{100}$

6. $\dfrac{?}{96} = \dfrac{14.2}{100}$

APPLICATIONS

7. Andy is a museum guide. He had already taken 76 of 95 students on tour of the museum. What percent of the students have not yet taken a tour? Use a proportion to solve.

8. Paula works at a wildlife beach refuge. 12.5% of the eggs a sea turtle lays hatch. Paula counts 22 of the baby turtles scrambling toward the ocean. How many eggs did the turtle lay? Use a proportion to solve.

9. Max buys a new set of small sockets marked $16.66. He gets a 10% discount through his employer. How much did Max have to pay for the sockets? Use a proportion to solve.

10. Lisa manages the school cafeteria. She tracks the lunch counts teachers send telling who will buy which plate. Today, students have a choice of chicken nuggets or fish sticks. 357 students want chicken nuggets. That is 75% of the total number of students who will buy cafeteria lunches. How many students will buy cafeteria lunches? How many will buy fish sticks? Use a proportion to solve.

11. Rita has an order to print 140 T-shirts. She has finished 120 of them. What percent of the job is finished? Use a proportion to solve.

12. Beverly is wallpapering a room with border that is 5 yards long. She has used 2.5 rolls and completed only 25% of the room. What is the total number of linear yards in the room? Beverly has 6 more rolls of wall border. Does she have enough to finish the room? If so, how much border is left over? If not, how much more border does Beverly need? Use a proportion to solve.

Check your answers on page 123.

CHAPTER 3 Summary

Finding the Part Based on the Percent and the Whole

A part of an amount is found by multiplying the whole amount by the decimal form of the percent. The whole times the percent equals the part.

EXERCISE A

Find the part in each of the following problems.

1. Find 15% of 60   **2.** Find 125% of 200   **3.** Find 45% of 90

Check your answers
on page 124.

Finding the Whole Based on the Percent and the Part

To find the whole if given the percent and the part, divide the part by the decimal form of the percent.

EXERCISE B

Find the wholes.

4. 28 is 25% of ?   **5.** 45 is 30% of ?

6. 311 is 80% of ?   **7.** 44.4 is 60% of ?

Check your answers
on page 124.

Using Percent to Find the Original Price

To find the original price, or whole amount, first find the difference between 100% and the percent of the discount. Then divide the price paid by the decimal form of the percent difference.

Find the original price.

8. Discount 30%
   Sale price $21

9. Discount 60%
   Sale price $5.61

Check your answers
on page 124.

10. Discount 25%
    Sale price $35

11. Discount 64%
    Sale price $212

Finding the Percent from the Part and the Whole

To find what percent a part of a number is of the whole, divide the part by the whole amount. Rename the decimal in the quotient as a percent.

EXERCISE D

Find the percent.

12. 8 is ? percent of 64

13. 6 is ? percent of 24

14. 48 is ? percent of 640

15. 27 is ? percent of 72

Check your answers
on page 124.

The Proportional Method to Solve Percent Problems

Any percent problem can be expressed as a proportion. Simply create a fraction with the part as numerator and the whole as denominator. Use the percent as the numerator of the second fraction, with 100 as the denominator. Once the problem is set up, "cross-multiply and divide."

$$\frac{part}{whole} = \frac{\%}{100}$$

EXERCISE E

Cross multiply and divide to find the missing value. Reduce the fractions to make your work easier whenever possible.

Check your answers
on page 124.

16. $\dfrac{24}{?} = \dfrac{30}{100}$

17. $\dfrac{120}{96} = \dfrac{?}{100}$

18. $\dfrac{?}{400} = \dfrac{30}{100}$

MATH AT WORK

1. **Business Owner** Tom owns a small restaurant. He has a budget of $526,408. His budget allows for 3% advertising. How much money will Tom spend on advertising?

2. **Hotel Manager** Gina manages the North Hills Inn. She finds that 96 of the rooms are booked for the weekend. The hotel will be 75% full. How many rooms does the hotel have in all?

3. **Picture Framer** A customer gives Joe a 40% coupon to pay for a picture frame. With the coupon, the frame costs $64.80. What was the original cost of the frame?

4. **Secretary** Elaine is a member of an office supply warehouse shopping club. She gets a 10% discount on everything she buys. Her bill before the discount was $59.60. How much did Elaine save?

5. **Clerk** Clayton makes a salary of $1,807.44 each month. $\frac{1}{3}$ of it is taken out for benefit payments and taxes. What is Clayton's take-home salary each month?

6. **Furniture Dealer** Carly advertises an antique armoire for $1600. She sells it for $1400. What percent of discount does Carly give on the armoire?

MATH AT WORK

7. **Business Owner** Eight of Aldo's employees are full time. This is 80% of his employees. How many employees work for Aldo?

8. **Sales Representative** Fred is a sales representative for a tool manufacturer. He is driving to visit a vendor that is 481 miles away. He plans on stopping for lunch after driving 60% of the way there. How many miles will Fred drive before stopping?

9. **Sales Representative** Renee works on commission. She has sold $498 dollars worth of equipment. It is 40% of the amount she needs before she starts earning her commission. How much equipment must Renee sell before earning a commission?

10. **Gymnastics Instructor** Lily teaches 27 gymnastic classes. She has 18% of all the classes taught. How many total classes are taught at the gymnastic center?

11. **Retail Clerk** Gail is a clerk in a store. She rings up a lamp that costs $56 on sale. It was recently marked 30% off. What was the price before it was marked down?

12. **Carpenter** Ed cut 2 feet off a board to make a shelf. This was 25% of the board. What was the total length of the board. How many more 2 foot long shelves can Ed cut?

13. Delivery Driver Angelo is delivering pizzas to a party. He has 1 vegetarian, 2 sausage, 2 cheese, and 4 pepperoni. What percent of the pizzas are pepperoni?

14. Advertising Distributor Nathan distributes flyers in neighborhoods. He has 2 packages of 250 flyers left to give out. He is 80% done. How many flyers was Nathan given to distribute?

15. Sales Manager An airline is having a promotional offer to reduce fares by 30%. If people call the first day, they get an additional 15% off. Jason books a trip the first day for $308 to visit the regional sales office. How much money does Jason save from the original price by booking the first day?

16. Retail Clerk A pet shop is having a 20% off sale on dog supplies. Jason sells a collie puppy for $69.80. Before the discount is applied, the customer buys $68.25 worth of dog supplies. What will be the cost of the dog and supplies after the discount is taken into account?

17. Photographer Laura is a school photographer. She has taken pictures of 27 classrooms at one school. She is $\frac{3}{4}$ done. How many classes must Laura photograph?

18. Custodian Belva pays cash to get a 10% discount on cleaning supplies. Her cost is $72.90. What was the original price?

19. Mason   Chris is building a 32 foot stone wall. He has completed 20 feet of it. What percent of the wall does Chris have left to build?

20. Painter   Otto is has a contract to paint 160 rooms. He has already painted 92 of them. What percent has he painted?

21. Network Manager   Keeno bought a computer program for $39.97. The original price was $52.50. What percent of discount did Keeno get on the program?

22. Curtain Maker   Cecila has 24 yards of material. She is sewing 2 sets of curtains that each require 9 yards of material. What percent of the fabric will be used for curtains?

23. Personnel Manager   Andrew has received 30 applications in response to an ad he placed in the paper. 20% of the applicants meet the educational qualifications for the job. But only $\frac{1}{2}$ of the educationally qualified applicants have the amount of experience Andrew is looking for. How many applicants meet the education and experience requirements?

24. Teacher   Linda is flying to a conference. She can buy a two week advanced purchased ticket for 40% less than the full-fare price. The full-fare ticket is $330. How much will Linda save by buying the ticket ahead of time?

Check your answers
on page 125.

CHAPTER 4

Interest

LESSON 17 The Meaning of Simple Interest

Mason is the bookkeeper of a small remodeling company. He is going over the company's latest financial statement.

Finding Interest Using the Interest Formula

The interest formula is as follows: $i = p \times r \times t$
interest = principal × annual interest rate × time (in years)

Mason is checking on the remodeling company's savings account. The company deposited $3,000 in a savings account with an annual **interest rate** of 7%. Mason wants to calculate how much **interest** the company will make if the money remains in the savings account for 1 year. To do this, Mason uses the interest formula.

EXAMPLE 1

$i = prt$ $i = \$3,000 \times 7\% \times 1 \text{ year}$

Step 1	Change the percent to a decimal.	**7% = .07**
Step 2	Multiply the principal amount by the interest rate: $3,000 × .07 = 210.	$3,000 × .07 $210.00
Step 3	Multiply the answer from step 2 by the time in years.	$210 × 1 $210

Find the interest.

1. $700 at 5% for 1 year

2. $5,000 at 6% for 1 year

3. $450 at 12% for 1 year

4. $1,300 at 9% for 1 year

APPLICATION

5. Mason is now figuring the amount of interest the company will need to pay for a short term bank loan. The company borrowed $8,000 at an annual interest rate of 8% for 1 year. How much interest will be paid on this loan?

Check your answers on page 127.

Finding Interest With a Mixed Number Percent

Sometimes the annual interest rate is a mixed number percent, such as $5\frac{1}{2}$%. When this occurs, change the mixed number percent into a decimal percent, then proceed as usual using the interest formula.

EXAMPLE 2

Find the interest on a $2,000 deposit at $5\frac{1}{2}$% for 1 year.

Step 1	Change the mixed number percent into a decimal percent: since the fraction $\frac{1}{2}$ equals the decimal .5.	$5\frac{1}{2}\% = 5.5\%$
Step 2	Change the percent to a decimal.	$5.5\% = .055$

Step 3 Multiply the three numbers together.

$$\begin{array}{r} \$3,000 \\ \times.055 \\ \hline 15000 \\ +150000 \\ \hline \$165.000 \end{array} \qquad \begin{array}{r} 165 \\ \times 1 \\ \hline \$165 \end{array}$$

EXERCISE 17B

Find the interest.

6. $400 at $6\frac{1}{2}$% for 1 year

7. $900 at $9\frac{3}{4}$% for 1 year

8. $6,000 at $8\frac{1}{4}$% for 1 year

9. $3,500 at $7\frac{3}{4}$% for 1 year

APPLICATION

10. The remodeling company is doing a large job for a doctor's office. It was agreed that the remodeling cost of $18,000 be financed at an annual interest rate of $11\frac{1}{2}$% for 1 year. Mason needs to figure how much interest the remodeling company will make on this loan to the doctor's office.

Check your answers
on page 127.

When calculating simple interest on a deposit or a loan, simply follow the interest formula; i = prt.

USE WHAT YOU HAVE LEARNED

Find the interest.

1. $875 at 11% for 1 year

2. $9,500 at 5% for 1 year

3. $360 at $3\frac{1}{2}$% for 1 year

4. $4,200 at $8\frac{1}{4}$% for 1 year

5. The Hardware Place deposited $6,500 into a savings account which has an annual interest rate of 6%. How much interest will they make if they leave the money in the savings account for 1 year?

6. Nan's Nursery deposited $8,000 in a CD at their bank for a period of one year. If the interest rate is $4\frac{1}{2}\%$, how much interest will the nursery make on their CD?

7. Samantha works for a furniture store. She just made a sale of $1,250 worth of living room furniture. The customer will be financing the $1,250 for 1 year at an interest rate of $15\frac{1}{2}\%$. How much interest will the customer pay for the furniture?

8. Geoff is a photographer who just received $1,500 from a publishing company for some of his photos. Geoff is going to deposit this money into a savings account which has a $5\frac{1}{4}\%$ interest rate. If Geoff leaves the money in the savings account for 1 year, how much total money will he have in the account at the end of the year?

9. Ramona is the manager of Hair By Us. She is working on the details of a $15,000 loan to cover the cost of some expansion & remodeling the salon is planning. If the loan is for 1 year at an interest rate of 9%, how much interest will the salon have to pay? What will be their monthly payment?

$$\text{Monthly Payment} = \frac{\text{loan amount} + \text{interest}}{\text{number of months}}$$

10. A construction company purchased a dump truck for $12,000. This amount is to be financed for 1 year at an interest rate of $13\frac{1}{2}\%$. How much interest will the construction company have to pay? What will be their monthly payment?

Check your answers on page 127.

LESSON 18   Simple Interest for More than a Year

Jessica owns a small flower shop. She would like to add on to the shop and needs to borrow some money to accomplish this.

Finding Interest for More than One Year

Sometimes money is used for periods of more than 1 year. The interest formula (i = prt) is still used; the "t" will be replaced by the amount of time in years.

Jessica is borrowing $12,000 to add on to her flower shop. The interest rate is 11% and the loan is for $3\frac{1}{2}$ years. To determine the amount of interest she will pay, Jessica uses the interest formula.

EXAMPLE 1

i = prt   i = $12,000 × 11% × 3$\frac{1}{2}$ years

Step 1   Change the percent to a decimal. 11% = .11

$$\begin{array}{r} \$12,000 \\ \times\ .11 \\ \hline 12000 \\ +120000 \\ \hline \$1,320.00 \end{array}$$

Step 2   Multiply the principal amount by the interest rate. $12,000 × .11 = $1,320

Step 3   Since the time in years is a mixed number, first change it to a decimal: $3\frac{1}{2}$ = 3.5. Now multiply the answer from Step 2 by the time in years. $1,320 × 3.5 = $4,620

$$\begin{array}{r} \$1,320 \\ \times\ 3.5 \\ \hline 6600 \\ +39600 \\ \hline \$4,620.0 \end{array}$$

EXERCISE 18

Find the interest.

1. $650 at 13% for 2 years

2. $8,000 at $6\frac{1}{2}$% for 5 years

3. $13,000 at 9% for $4\frac{1}{2}$ years

4. $2,700 at $5\frac{1}{2}$% for $1\frac{1}{2}$ years

APPLICATION

5. Jessica is thinking about cashing in her bank CD in order to help with the flower shop addition. She deposited $6,000 in a 2 year CD at a $7 \frac{3}{4}$% interest rate. How much interest will this CD make?

Check your answers on page 128.

When calculating simple interest on a deposit or a loan of more than 1 year, simply replace the "t" in the interest formula with the number of years.

USE WHAT YOU HAVE LEARNED

Find the interest.

1. $1,600 at 9% for $3 \frac{1}{4}$ years

2. $950 at $4 \frac{3}{4}$% for 2 years

3. $1,280 at 15% for $5 \frac{1}{2}$ years

4. $1,400 at 7% for $4 \frac{3}{4}$ years

5. $560 at $3 \frac{1}{4}$% for $1 \frac{1}{2}$ years

6. $18,000 at $11 \frac{1}{2}$% for $8 \frac{1}{2}$ years

APPLICATIONS

7. Fred is the owner of a Christmas tree farm. The Christmas season has just ended and Fred has $15,500 to deposit in the business savings account. If the savings account earns $5\frac{3}{4}\%$ interest and Fred leaves the money in for 3 years, how much interest will he make?

8. Cheryl is the office manager of an insurance agency. She just received her end of the year bonus of $200. If Cheryl deposits this money into a CD for $1\frac{1}{2}$ years with an interest rate of $6\frac{3}{4}\%$, how much interest will she make?

9. A storage complex is adding 20 new storage units to accommodate more tenants. Marc, the manager of the storage complex, is figuring the cost of the new units. If $10,500 is borrowed at an interest rate of 12% for 4 years, how much interest will be paid? What will the monthly payment be?

10. Ricardo just sold a compact car to a customer for $16,700. The customer will be making a $900 down-payment on the car. If the balance is to be financed for 5 years at an interest rate of $9\frac{1}{4}\%$, how much interest will the customer pay?

11. Ricardo received a commission check this week of $400 for his car sales. If Ricardo puts this money into a savings account for $1\frac{1}{2}$ years at an interest rate of $4\frac{1}{2}\%$, how much interest will he make?

12. A remodeling company purchased a paint spraying machine for $9,250. A down-payment of $550 was made. If the balance is to be financed for $2\frac{1}{2}$ years at an interest rate of 12%, how much interest will the remodeling company pay? What will the monthly payment be for the paint spraying machine?

Check your answers
on page 129.

LESSON 19 Simple Interest for Less than a Year

Rosa works for an appliance store. When her customers make large purchases, they often finance the amount of the purchase.

Sometimes money is used for periods of less than 1 year. In these cases a decimal or a fraction will be used for the amount of time in the interest formula. For example, if the time given is 6 months, show this as the fraction $\frac{6}{12}$ (the numerator—6—is the number of months given; the denominator is always 12 since there are 12 months in a year). Reduce the fraction $\frac{6}{12}$ to $\frac{1}{2}$ and change it into the decimal 0.5.

Finding Interest for Less than One Year

Rosa just sold a refrigerator to a customer for $1,150. The customer chose to finance this amount for 8 months at an interest rate of 12%. To determine the amount of interest the customer will pay, Rosa uses the interest formula.

EXAMPLE 1

i = prt   i = $1150 × 12% × 8 months

Step 1 Change the percent to a decimal.
12% = .12

$$\begin{array}{r} \$1{,}150 \\ \times\ .12 \\ \hline 2300 \\ +11500 \\ \hline \$138.00 \end{array}$$

Step 2   Multiply the principal amount by the interest rate. $1,150 × .12 = $138

Step 3 Since the time is less than 1 year, write it as a fraction: $\frac{8}{12}$. Reduce the fraction: $\frac{8}{12} = \frac{2}{3}$. Since you cannot change $\frac{2}{3}$ into a simple decimal, multiply the answer from step 2 by the fraction $\frac{2}{3}$.

$$\frac{\$138}{1} \times \frac{2}{3} = \$92$$

EXERCISE 19

Find the interest.

1. $780 at 11% for 6 months

2. $5,200 at $7\frac{1}{2}$% for 3 months

3. $11,000 at 8% for 9 months

4. $1,600 at 6% for 7 months

APPLICATION

5. Rosa sold a washer and dryer to a customer at a total cost of $960. The customer is financing this purchase for 10 months at an interest rate of 10%. How much interest will the customer pay on this purchase?

Check your answers on page 130.

When calculating simple interest on a deposit or a loan of less than 1 year, use a decimal or fraction for the "t" in the interest formula.

USE WHAT YOU HAVE LEARNED

Find the interest.

1. $1,900 at 6% for 4 months

2. $400 at $2\frac{3}{4}$% for 6 months

3. $1,650 at 16% for 2 months

4. $1,800 at 5% for 8 months

5. $800 at $7\frac{1}{2}$% for 10 months

6. $10,000 at 12% for 5 months

APPLICATIONS

7. Corrine runs a daycare out of her home. She is borrowing $2,000 from her bank to remodel the play room. Corrine is borrowing the money for 9 months at an interest rate of 12%. How much interest will she pay on the loan?

8. Cynthia is a photographer. She bought some new camera equipment for $900. She is financing the purchase for 5 months at an interest rate of 8%. How much interest will Cynthia pay?

9. Max works as an insurance agent. He just received an advance of $360. He decides to deposit the money into a 6 month CD. How much interest will Max make on this money if the interest rate is 7%?

10. Alex works at a music store. His customer just bought a used piano for $1,500. A $250 down-payment was made. The balance is to be paid in 10 months at an interest rate of 12%. How much interest will the customer pay? What will the monthly payment be on the piano?

11. Alex receives a commission check of $320 for the month. He decides to put this money into a 3 month CD which has a 5% interest rate. How much total money (principal and interest) will Alex have in the CD at the end of 3 months?

12. Alice is the office manager at a doctor's office. They just purchased a new computer system for a total cost of $3,500. Alice is figuring what the monthly payment will be on the new system. A $300 down-payment was made and the balance will be paid in 4 months. If the interest rate is $9\frac{3}{4}\%$, how much interest will the doctor pay? What will the monthly payment be for the computer?

Check your answers on page 130.

LESSON 20 Compound Interest

Winston received a commission of $500 this month from the car dealership he works for. He is thinking about putting this money into a savings account.

Banks and savings institutions pay **compound interest**. Compound interest is interest paid on the principal plus the interest already accumulated. Consider $100 at 10%, compounded **annually**. At the end of the first year, the principal ($100) plus the interest ($100 × .1 = $10) equals $110 ($100 + $10 = $110). This $110 becomes the new principal. The second year's interest is 10% of $110, or $11 ($110 × .1 = $11). This amount of interest is added to the principal to create a new principal for the next year ($110 + $11 = $121). Even though the interest rate (10%) stays the same, the principal and the amount of interest increase each year.

Finding Compound Interest

Winston may deposit his $500 commission check into a savings account at a bank that pays 6% annual interest, compounded annually. Winston wants to compute how much money he will have in the bank if he leaves the money in for 2 years. To do this, Winston uses the interest formula twice.

EXAMPLE 1

Find the total of a $500 deposit at 6%, compounded annually, for 2 years.

Step 1 Find the interest for the first year.
$500 × .06 × 1 = $30

$$\begin{array}{r} \$500 \\ \times .06 \\ \hline \$30.00 \end{array}$$

$30 × 1 = $30

Step 2 Add the interest from the first year to the original principal amount.
$500 + $30 = $530

$$\begin{array}{r} \$500 \\ + \$30 \\ \hline \$530 \end{array}$$

Step 3 Use the new principal amount to compute the interest for the second year. $530 × .06 × 1 = $31.80

$$\begin{array}{r} \$530 \\ \times .06 \\ \hline \$31.80 \end{array}$$

$31.80 × 1 = $31.80

Step 4 Add the second year's earned interest to the new principal.
$530 + $31.80 = $561.80

$$\begin{array}{r} \$530.00 \\ + \$31.80 \\ \hline \$561.80 \end{array}$$

EXERCISE 20A

Find the total.

1. $180 at 5% for 2 years

2. $1,200 at 4% for 2 years

3. $700 at 6% for 2 years

4. $400 at $5\frac{1}{2}$% for 2 years

APPLICATION

5. Winston heard about a credit union that pays a 7% interest rate, compounded annually. He wants to find out how much more he would make if he deposited his $500 commission check into the credit union for 2 years, rather than at the bank. Calculate the total amount Winston will have if he deposits his check into the credit union.

Check your answers on page 131.

Finding Interest Compounded Other Than Annually

Sometimes interest is compounded **semiannually** (twice a year), quarterly (four times a year), or daily. To compute earned interest compounded more than once a year, follow the same procedure.

EXAMPLE 2

Find the total for 1 year of $300 at 4%, compounded semiannually.

Step 1	Find the interest earned for the first 6 months. 6 months is half (.5) a year. $300 \times .04 \times .5 = 6$	$300 $\times .04$ $12.00	$12 $\times .5$ $6.0
Step 2	Add the interest from the first 6 months to the original principal.	$300 + $6 = $306	
Step 3	Use the new principal amount to compute the interest for the second 6 months. $306 \times .04 \times .5 = 6.12$	$306 $\times .04$ $12.24	$12.24 $\times .5$ $6.120
Step 4	Add the interest from the second 6 months to the current principal.	$306 + $6.12 = $312.12	

Find the total.

6. $300 at 8%, compounded semiannually, for 1 year

7. $1,000 at 6%, compounded semiannually, for 1 year

8. $800 at 4%, compounded semiannually, for 1 year

9. $2,000 at 3%, compounded semiannually, for 1 year

APPLICATION

10. Bernice, a legal assistant, just finished a big project for her boss. She received a $200 bonus for her hard work. Bernice wants to deposit the $200 into a CD with an annual interest rate of 6%, compounded semiannually. How much total money will Bernice have in the CD at the end of 1 year?

Check your answers on page 132.

USE WHAT YOU HAVE LEARNED

Find the total.

1. $550 at 8%, compounded annually, for 2 years

2. $1,600 at $5\frac{1}{2}$%, compounded annually, for 2 years

3. $100 at 4%, compounded semiannually, for 1 year

4. $1,400 at 6%, compounded semiannually, for 1 year

5. Marc received an advance from the insurance company he works for. Marc wants to deposit the $350 check into a savings account. The account has an interest rate of 4%, compounded annually. If Marc keeps the money in the account for 2 years, how much money will be in the account at the end of 2 years?

6. Ruth is the manager of a women's clothing store. She received a commission check of $250 for sales she made. Ruth deposits the $250 check into a CD at an interest rate of 8%, compounded semiannually, for 1 year. How much money will Ruth have in the CD at the end of the year?

7. Lisa received her Christmas bonus of $100. She wants to deposit this into a savings account which earns 7% interest, compounded annually. If she leaves this money in the account for 2 years, how much total money will be in the account?

8. Chuck sold some of his hand-made furniture at a peddler's show last weekend. Chuck made $3,250 at the show. He wants to take $2,000 of his earnings and deposit it into a savings account. If Chuck's bank pays a $5 \frac{1}{2}$% interest rate, compounded annually, and Chuck leaves his money in the account for 2 years, how much money will he have?

9. Chrissy, a secretary for a small retail store, sold her home computer to her boss for $900. Chrissy took half of that money and put it in a CD which earns 8% interest, compounded semiannually. How much money will Chrissy have at the end of 1 year?

10. This quarter, Frank received commissions of $210, $240, and $150 from the furniture store he works for. Frank wants to deposit his commissions into a savings account that pays 6% interest, compounded semiannually. If Frank deposits all his commissions into this account, how much will he have at the end of 1 year?

Check your answers on page 132.

CHAPTER 1 Summary

Finding Interest Using the Interest Formula

Interest is a fee paid for the use of money. The interest formula is as follows: i = prt, where interest = principal × annual interest rate × time (in years).

EXERCISE A

Find the interest.

1. $400 at 6% for 1 year

2. $600 at $4\frac{3}{4}$% for 1 year

3. $4,000 at $5\frac{1}{4}$% for 1 year

4. $2,500 at $8\frac{3}{4}$% for 1 year

Check your answers on page 133.

Finding Interest for More Than One Year

Sometimes money is used for periods of more than 1 year. The interest formula (i = prt) is still used; the "t" will be replaced by the amount of time in years.

EXERCISE B

Find the interest.

4. $1,200 at 6% for $1\frac{1}{4}$ years

5. $750 at $5\frac{3}{4}$% for 2 years

6. $1,160 at 12% for $3\frac{1}{2}$ years

7. $1,700 at 6% for $2\frac{3}{4}$ years

Check your answers on page 133.

Finding Interest for More Than One Year

Sometimes money is used for periods of less than 1 year. The interest formula (i = prt) is still used; the "t" is replaced by the fraction of a year. A month is $\frac{1}{12}$ of a year.

EXERCISE C

Find the interest.

8. $1,500 at 5% for 6 months

9. $600 at $3\frac{2}{5}$% for 3 months

10. $1,150 at 12% for 9 months

11. $96 at 15% for 8 months

Check your answers
on page 134.

Compound Interest

To compound interest, use the interest formula to compute the **annual** interest, add the interest accrued to the principal, and then **recompute** the interest for the new balance. Do this as many times as **necessary**.

EXERCISE D

Find the total.

12. $45 at 7%, compounded annually, for 2 years

13. $1,200 at $4\frac{1}{2}$%, compounded annually, for 2 years

14. $1400 at 6%, compounded semiannually, for 1 year

15. $200 at 5%, compounded semiannually, for 2 years

Check your answers
on page 134.

1. **Heating and Air-Conditioning Technician** Energy Mizer, an air conditioning/heating system maintenance company, deposited $8,500 into a savings account with an annual interest rate of $3\frac{3}{4}$%. How much interest will they make in one year?

2. **Automobile Dealer** Yancy works in a automobile dealership. His customer wants to buy a $16,500 car with $2,000 down. This customer qualifies for financing the balance at $7\frac{1}{2}$% per year for five years. What is the total simple interest the customer will pay?

3. **Accountant** Cheryl, the accountant, has saved $4,375 in a savings account which pays 3.5% interest. How much will she earn in one year?

4. **Carpenter** Geoffrey has just received $2,000 for a job he completed. He can either deposit it in a savings account with 3.5% simple interest or in a CD with 3.5% interest compounded semi-annually? Which account will bear him more interest?

5. **Purchasing Agent** Cynthia must purchase a new photocopy machine for the company. The machine costs $1,059.95. As the company has good credit, it can be financed at 4.25% over two years. How much interest will they pay?

6. **Small Business Owner** How much interest can Mary earn by depositing $5,135 of her shop's profits for 6 months at 3.9% interest?

MATH AT WORK

7. **Data-Entry Clerk** Jennie's office bought a new computer at $2,599.95. They paid $500 down and financed the rest at 12% over 10 months. What were their monthly payments?

8. **Line Worker** The Employees' Credit Union is offering savings accounts with 4.9% interest per year. How much will Phil earn if he puts $1,500 in this account?

9. **Financial Officer** Clancy's company wants to earn at least $100 in interest on savings. If he invests $2,000 at 4.75% for one year, will he reach this goal?

10. **Buyer** John wants to purchase $5,000 worth of inventory in preparation for the busy season. If he borrows this at 11.5% per year, how much interest will he pay if he repays the loan in six months?

11. **Small Business Owner** Anne's boutique purchases $7,500 of Christmas ornaments with a small business loan of 9.9% per year. She is able to repay the loan in three months. How much does she repay?

12. **Payroll Clerk** Mrs. Jones, who works in the payroll department, deposited $10,000 in a savings account at $4\frac{1}{4}$% interest in January. She withdrew this money with interest at the end of November for Christmas bonuses. How much did she withdraw?

13. **Small Business Owner** Fred must decide which bank to place his company profits in. He can either deposit his $35,500 in Bank A at 3.5% simple interest or Bank B at 4.5% compounded interest. In which bank will he earn more Interest?

14. **Finance Officer** Samantha has just switched her company's savings to a new bank which compounds interest quarterly. She has deposited $6,000 at 4.5%. How much will her company have in the bank in 6 months?

15. **Salesperson** Frank earned commission checks or $300, $279, and $157. He deposited them in a savings account at 5% interest compounded semi-annually. How much did he have in his account at the end of the year?

16. **Food Processor** A canning factory just purchased a new labeling machine for $2,335.99 with 10% down and the balance on loan at 12% over 2 years. How much is their monthly payment?

17. **Messenger** Benny's Delivery Service made a $2,700 down payment on a $12,000.00 truck. They financed the balance at 12% over three years. What was their monthly payment?

18. **Office Manager** Fran, office manager for a group of doctors, just bought a new computer and printer for $4,299.00. They paid 20% down and financed the rest at $9\frac{3}{4}$% per year. If they pay it off in 3 months, how much interest will they have paid?

19. **Ice Cream Manufacturer** Ivan's Ice Cream Company will loan employees up to $1,000 at 3% per year. If 5 employees take out $1,000 loans, how much interest will Ivan's company receive at the end of one year?

20. **Contractor** Home Remodelers Inc. will allow customers to pay on installments with interest. Family A paid $12,000 upon receipt of bill. Family B paid $5,000 down and $3,000 at 2% per year and paid it in 6 months. Family C paid $3,000 down and paid $6,000 at 3% over 12 months. How much interest did Home Remodelers earn?

21. **Artisan** Frames Unlimited deposits net income quarterly in its savings account which earns 5% interest compounded quarterly. If they started the year with $1,000 and deposited $500 each quarter, how much will they have at the end of the year?

22. **Artisan** How much of Frames Unlimited's balance (in problem 21) was interest?

23. **Real Estate Agent** Al's client purchases a piece of real estate for $10,000 at 8.75% over 3 years? What is the total cost of the land to the client?

24. **Auto-Body Technician** Joe's Auto Body Shop had one loan for $2,000 at 7% and another for $3,500 at 9%. How much would the monthly payments be on a debt consolidation loan at 7% over 2 years?

Check your answers on page 134.

ANSWER KEY

CHAPTER 1 Introduction to Percent

LESSON 1 Parts of a Whole   pages 1-4

EXERCISE 1

1. Martha is late less often than most workers. **Martha was late for work** $\frac{3}{250}$ **= .012, or 1.2% of the days.** The company wide rate for tardiness is 2.3% or .023. .012 is less than .023.

2. No. Bryon's stamping machine is still performing well enough. Bill's machine is turning out $\frac{4 \text{ reject parts}}{1000 \text{ parts}}$ = .004 reject. This is 0.4% ($\frac{4}{10}$ of 1%). He doesn't report the machine until the reject rate exceeds 3%.

3. Melanie did more of her quota. 23% = .23 $\frac{1}{5}$ = .20 .23 is greater than .20

4. $\frac{3}{10}$ = 30% $\frac{5}{10}$ = 50% $\frac{7}{10}$ = 70% $\frac{9}{10}$ = 90%

USE WHAT YOU HAVE LEARNED

1. 44% $\frac{1}{3}$ = .3$\overline{33}$ .437 = .437 44% = . 440

2. $\frac{2}{3}$ $\frac{2}{3}$ = .6$\overline{66}$ .654 = .654 66% = .660

3. .42 $\frac{2}{5}$ = .40 .42 = .42 40% = .40

4. 88% $\frac{3}{4}$ = .750 .875 = .875 88% = .880

5. $\frac{2}{5}$ = .4 4% = .04

6. .4200 = 42% $\frac{4}{2}$ = 2.0

7. $\frac{5}{8}$ = .625 .58 = .58

8. $\frac{4}{5}$ = 80% .45 = .45

9. No, Rochelle is on-time a little less often this year than last. **Last year, 3 out of 4 flights she was on arrived on time.** $\frac{3}{4}$ **= .75, or 75% compared to 70% this year.**

10. Yes, Dan's salary represents 33% of his income. $\frac{\$125}{\$375}$ = $\frac{1}{3}$ = .333, or 33%

11. No, Sonia needs 10 more single rooms. 50% = .5 She set aside 150 × .5 = 75 rooms. 85 people asked for single rooms.

12. Brad has been assigned more rooms than he is supposed to have. $\frac{6 \text{ rooms}}{20 \text{ rooms}}$ = .3, or 30%

13. Brett is getting less preparation time than he should. $\dfrac{1 \text{ hour}}{8 \text{ hours}} = .125$, or 13% His contract calls for 15%.

14. The ramp has less than a 14% grade. $\dfrac{2 \text{ feet}}{16 \text{ feet}} = .125$, or 13%

LESSON 2 The Meaning of Percent

pages 5-9

EXERCISE 2A

1. Shift 1 had the highest percentage of defects.

Shift 1	Shift 2
$\dfrac{400 \text{ defects}}{6000 \text{ nozzles}} = .06\overline{66}$	$\dfrac{200 \text{ defects}}{5000 \text{ nozzles}} = .04$

$$\begin{array}{r} .07 \\ \times\,100 \\ \hline 7\% \end{array} \qquad \begin{array}{r} .04 \\ \times\,100 \\ \hline 4\% \end{array}$$

2. The increase is 50%. 3,000 cars is half of 6,000 cars, so the new figure, 9,000 cars, is half again more than the original figure, 6,000 cars.

EXERCISE 2B

3. 114 represents the part of the plane that's filled
120 represents the whole capacity of the plane.
95% describes the relationship between the part and the whole.

4. 75 represents the part of her time that she can travel.
250 represents the whole number of working days in a year.
30% describes the relationship between the part and the whole.

5. You need the traffic flow for 1992. This figure represents the whole.

USE WHAT YOU HAVE LEARNED

1. 65% is the percent, 106 is the whole, and the question asks you for the part.

2. 40% is the percent, $64.80 is the part, and the question asks you for the whole.

3. $59.60 is the part, $65.50 is the whole, and the question asks you for the percent.

4. $1,928 is the part, 25% is the percent, and the question asks you for the whole.

5. $1,600 is the whole, $1,400 is the part, and the question asks you for the percent.

6. 60% is the percent, 12 is the part, and the question asks you for the whole.

1. $84\% = 0.84$ **2.** $45\% = 0.45$ **3.** $13\% = 0.13$ **4.** $5\% = 0.05\%$

Move the decimal point two places to the left to change the percent into a decimal.

5. $15\% = 0.15$ The question asks you to change the percent (15%) to a decimal.

6. $0.12 = 12\%$ **7.** $0.68 = 68\%$ **8.** $0.75 = 75$ **9.** $0.01 = 1\%$

Move the decimal point two places to the right to change the decimal into a percent.

10. $0.91 = 91\%$ The question asks you to change the decimal (0.91) to a percent.

1. $89\% = 0.89$ **2.** $40\% = 0.4$ **3.** $92\% = 0.92$ **4.** $3\% = 0.03$

Move the decimal point two places to the left to change the percent into a decimal.

5. $0.79 = 79\%$ **6.** $0.32 = 32\%$ **7.** $0.07 = 7\%$ **8.** $0.53 = 53\%$

Move the decimal point two places to the right to change the decimal into a percent.

9. $30\% = 0.3$ The question asks you to change the percent (30%) to a decimal.

10. $0.08 = 8\%$ The question asks you to change the decimal (0.08) to a percent.

11. $0.35 \times 7{,}500 = 2{,}625$ The question asks you to determine what 35% is of her total sales: $2{,}625 + 50 + 50 = 2{,}725$. The question asks you to determine her total earnings, adding up her commission (2,625) and her two bonuses (50 each).

12. $0.49 = 49\%$ The question asks you to change the decimal (0.49) to a percent. $0.23 = 23\%$ The question asks you to change the decimal (0.23) to a percent.

13. $0.05 \times 855 = 42$ The question asks you to determine what 5% is of the number of rooms in the hotel (855).

14. The question asks you to determine the difference between the profits from last year and those from this year: $400{,}000 - 350{,}000 = 50{,}000$ The question asks you to determine what percent the increase (50,000) is of last year's profits (350,000): $\dfrac{50{,}000}{350{,}000} = 14\%$.

EXERCISE 4 _____

1. $\dfrac{4}{9} = 44\%$ 2. $\dfrac{13}{25} = 52\%$ 3. $\dfrac{31}{115} = 27\%$ 4. $\dfrac{127}{349} = 36\%$

Change the fraction into a decimal by dividing the numerator by the denominator. Move the decimal point two places to the right to change the decimal into a percent.

5. $65 + 290 = 355$. The question asks you to add his hourly wage (65) to his tips (290). $\dfrac{65}{355} = 18\%$ The question asks you to determine what percent his hourly wage (65) is of his total earnings.

USE WHAT YOU HAVE LEARNED _____

1. $\dfrac{5}{9} = 56\%$ 2. $\dfrac{3}{7} = 43\%$ 3. $\dfrac{8}{27} = 30\%$ 4. $\dfrac{3}{61} = 5\%$

5. $\dfrac{12}{91} = 13\%$ 6. $\dfrac{26}{73} = 36\%$ 7. $\dfrac{57}{283} = 20\%$ 8. $\dfrac{139}{765} = 18\%$

Change the fraction into a decimal by dividing the numerator by the denominator. Move the decimal point two places to the right to change the decimal into a percent.

9. $\dfrac{1}{47} = 2\%$ The question asks you to determine what percent the dollar is of his tips (47). Yes, he did give the busboy enough.

10. $\dfrac{19}{29} = 66\%$ The question asks you to determine what percent her profit (19) is of the amount she sells each basket for (29).

11. $\dfrac{639}{1528} = 42\%$ The question asks you to determine what percent her Christmas sales (639) were of the entire year's sales (1,528) $\dfrac{467}{1528} = 31\%$ The question asks you to determine what percent her Mother's Day sales (467) were of the entire year's sales (1,528).

12. $\dfrac{26}{500} = 5\%$ The question asks you to determine what percent the damaged ornaments (26) are of the entire shipment (500).

13. Yes, the price increase does make up for the rising costs. $14.95 - 12.95 = 2$ The question asks you to determine the difference between the old price (12.95) and the new price (14.95). $\dfrac{2}{12.95} = 15\%$ The question asks you to determine what percent the price increase (2) is of the old price (12.95).

14. $\dfrac{3}{52} = 6\%$ The question asks you to determine what percent of her total sales (52) were size small (3). $\dfrac{10}{52} = 19\%$ The question asks you to determine what percent of her total sales (52) were size medium (10). $\dfrac{19}{52} = 37\%$ The question asks you to determine what percent of her total sales (52) were size large

(19). $\frac{20}{52} = 38\%$ The question asks you to determine what percent of her total sales (52) were size extra large (20). $0.06 \times 200 = 12$ The question asks you to determine what the percent of small T-shirts (6%) is of her next order (200). $0.19 \times 200 = 38$ The question asks you to determine what the percent of medium T-shirts (19%) is of her next order (200). $0.37 \times 200 = 74$ The question asks you to determine what the percent of large T-shirts (37%) is of her next order (200). $0.38 \times 200 = 76$ The question asks you to determine what the percent of extra large T-shirts (38%) is of her next order (200).

LESSON 5 Percent Larger Than 100%   pages 16-19

EXERCISE 5A

1. 129%=1.29   **2.** 590%= 5.9   **3.** 234%= 2.34   **4.** 101%= 1.01

Move the decimal point two places to the left to change the percent to a decimal.

5. $1.03 \times 150 = 155$ The question asks you to determine what 103% of the maximum capacity (150) is.

EXERCISE 5B

6. 5.29 = 529%   **7.** 2.93 = 293%   **8.** 3.67 = 367%.   **9.** 8.36 = 836%

Move the decimal point two places to the right to change the decimal to a percent.

10. 1.02 = 102% The question asks you to change the decimal (1.02) to a percent.

EXERCISE 5C

11. $4\frac{1}{2} = 4.5 = 450\%$ **12.** $1\frac{2}{3} = 1.666 = 167\%$

13. $9\frac{9}{10} = 9.9 = 990\%$ **14.** $2\frac{3}{4} = 2.75 = 275\%$

Convert the fraction to a decimal, and then convert the decimal to a percent.

15. $\frac{138}{130} = 106\%$ The question asks you to determine what percent of the flight is booked. This means that it is 6% overbooked.

USE WHAT YOU HAVE LEARNED

1. 405% = 4.05   **2.** 120% = 1.2   **3.** 238% = 2.38   **4.** 672% = 6.72

Move the decimal point two places to the left to change the percent to a decimal.

5. 1.49 = 149%   **6.** 8.99 = 899%   **7.** 7.51 = 751%   **8.** 9.11 = 911%

Move the decimal point two places to the right to change the decimal to a percent.

9. $2\frac{4}{5} = 2.8 = 280\%$ **10.** $5\frac{4}{9} = 5.444 = 544\%$

11. $8\dfrac{2}{3} = 8.666 = 867\%$ 12. $6\dfrac{1}{9} = 6.111 = 611\%$

Convert the fraction to a decimal, and then convert the decimal to a percent.

13. $\dfrac{11}{10} = 110\%$ The question asks you to determine what percent the amount of seed he poured in (11) is of the capacity of the bin (10).

14. $1.5 \times 50 = 75$ The question asks you to determine what 150% of the number of bags she ordered (50) is.

15. $\dfrac{15}{12} = 125\%$ The question asks you to determine what percent the order (15) is of his stock (12).

16. $\dfrac{30}{10} = 300\%$ The question asks you to determine what percent the price of the bookcase ($30) is of the cost ($10).

17. $\dfrac{2,193}{1,349} = 163\%$ The question asks you to determine what percent today's profits ($2,193) are of the average daily profits ($1,349).

18. $\dfrac{685}{600} = 114\%$ The question asks you to determine what percent the number of people showing up (685) is of the banquet hall's maximum capacity (600). This would be 14% over maximum capacity.

LESSON 6 Percent Smaller Than 1%   pages 20-23

EXERCISE 6A

1. $0.5\% = 0.005$ 2. $0.09\% = 0.0009$

3. $0.16\% = 0.0016$ 4. $0.021\% = 0.00021$

Move the decimal point two places to the left to change the percent to a decimal.

5. $0.1\% = 0.001$ The question asks you to change the percent (0.1%) to a decimal. Brad should tell the patient that his test may fail only one out a thousand times.

EXERCISE 6B

6. $0.007 = 0.7\%$ 7. $0.0071 = 0.71\%$

8. $0.0003 = 0.03\%$ 9. $0.00038 = 0.038\%$

Move the decimal point two places to the right to change the decimal to a percent.

10. 0.01% failure $1 - 0.9999 = 0.0001$ The question asks you to determine the difference between one and the failure rate (0.9999). $0.0001 = 0.01\%$ The question asks you to change the decimal (0.0001) to a percent.

EXERCISE 6C

11. $\dfrac{2}{984} = 0.002 = 0.2\%$ 12. $\dfrac{11}{12,937} = 0.00085 = 0.085\%$

13. $\dfrac{3}{682} = 0.0044 = 0.44\%$ **14.** $\dfrac{27}{15,835} = 0.0017 = 0.17\%$

Divide to change the fraction to a decimal. Move the decimal point two places to the right to change the decimal to a percent.

15. .03% failed $\dfrac{3}{11,254} = 0.0003$ The question asks you to change the fraction $\left(\dfrac{3}{11,254}\right)$ to a decimal. $0.0003 = 0.03\%$. The question asks you to change the decimal (0.0003) to a percent.

USE WHAT YOU HAVE LEARNED

1. $0.8\% = 0.008$ **2.** $0.08\% = 0.0008$

3. $0.019\% = 0.00019$ **4.** $0.71\% = 0.0071$

Move the decimal point two places to the left to change the percent to a decimal.

5. $0.0005 = 0.05\%$ **6.** $0.005 = 0.5\%$

7. $0.00026 = 0.026\%$ **8.** $0.0026 = 0.26\%$

Move the decimal point two places to the right to change the decimal to a percent.

9. $\dfrac{1}{999} = 0.001 = 0.1\%$ **10.** $\dfrac{18}{9,157} = 0.002 = 0.2\%$

11. $\dfrac{29}{9,782} = 0.003 = 0.3\%$ **12.** $\dfrac{327}{98,644} = 0.003 = 0.3\%$

Divide to change the fraction to a decimal. $0.003 = 0.3\%$. Move the decimal point two places to the right to change the decimal to a percent.

13. $\dfrac{4}{5,000} = 0.08\%$ The question asks you to determine what percent the broken glasses (4) are of the entire shipment (5,000).

14. $\dfrac{1}{100,000} = 0.001\%$ The question asks you to determine what percent the allowed impure substances (1) are in a given beverage (100,000).

15. She should tell the customer the alarm system fails only 3 times out of every 10,000 instances. $0.03\% = \dfrac{3}{10,000}$ The question asks you to change the percent (0.03%) to a fraction.

16. $\dfrac{21}{1,500} = 1.4\%$ The question asks you to determine what percent the returned mail (21) is of the entire mailing (1,500).

17. $\dfrac{4}{5,124} = 0.078\%$ The question asks you to determine what percent the flawed copies (4) are of the entire order (5,124). $0.00078 \times 15,000 = 12$ The question asks you to determine what 0.078% is of 15,000 copies.

18. $\dfrac{3}{850} = 0.35\%$ The question asks you to determine what percent the ruined photographs (3) are of the past 850. $0.01 \times 850 = 9$, to the nearest whole number. The question asks you to determine what one percent of 850 photographs would be. $9 - 3 = 6$ The question asks you to determine the difference between the amount of ruined photographs she had (3) and what she would have needed (9) to get the machine repaired.

CHAPTER 1 Summary   pages 24-26

EXERCISE A

1. 14% is the smallest of the set.

$\dfrac{1}{4} = .25$ 14% = .14

2. .3 is the smallest of the set.

33% = .33 $\dfrac{1}{3} = .3\overline{3}$

3. $\dfrac{3}{5}$ is the smallest of the set.

80% = .8 $\dfrac{3}{5} = .6$

4. .3% is the smallest of the set.

$\dfrac{3}{10} = .3$ .3% = .003

If you have trouble, refer to Lesson 1.

EXERCISE B

5. 72 represents the part, 120 represents the whole, and 60% represents the percent.

If you have trouble, refer to Lesson 2.

EXERCISE C

6. $.84 = 84 \times .01$ 7. $.45 = 45 \times .01$ 8. $.13 = 13 \times .01$ 9. $.05 = 5 \times .01$

If you have trouble, refer to Lesson 3.

EXERCISE D

10. 62.5% $\dfrac{5}{8} = 5 \div 8 = .625$ $.625 \times 100 = 62.5$

11. 33% $\dfrac{11}{33} = 11 \div 33 = .333$ $.333 \times 100 = 33.3 = 33.3$

12. 87.5% $\dfrac{56}{64} = 56 \div 64 = .875$ $.875 \times 100 = 87.5$

13. .67% $\dfrac{72}{108} = 72 \div 108 = .666$ $.666 \times 100 = 66.6 = 67$

If you have trouble, refer to Lesson 4.

EXERCISE E

14. 103% $1.03 \times 100 = 103$

15. .13% $.0013 \times 100 = .13$

16. 303.4% $3.034 \times 100 = 303.4$

17. 125% $\dfrac{25}{20} = 25 \div 20 = 1.25$ $1.25 \times 100 = 125$

If you have trouble, refer to Lessons 5 and 6.

1. $\dfrac{\$\,50,000}{\$145,000} = .34 = 34\%$

2. $\$8,250 \times 25\% = \$8,250 \times .25 = \$2,052.50$
$$3 \times \$50 \ = \ \underline{+150.00}$$
Total earnings $= \$2,202.50$

3. $.34 = 34\%$ $\$250,500 \times .34 \ = \ \$\,85,170.00$ Mexican Beer
$.48 = 48\%$ $\$250,500 \times .48 \ = \ \$120,240.00$ German Beer
$.18 = 18\%$ $\$250,500 \times .18 \ = \ \$\,45,090.00$ British Ale

4. $723 + 455 = 1,178$
$\dfrac{723}{1,178} = .61 = 61\%$ were sold at Christmas
$\dfrac{455}{1,178} = .39 = 39\%$ were sold at Mother's Day

5. $\dfrac{286}{10,000} = .0286 = .03 = 3\%$

6. $10,000$ ornaments $\times \$2.95$ each $= \$29,500.00$
$\$29,500 \times .03 = \$885.00 =$ damaged goods.

7. 111 delivered $- 100$ ordered $= 11$ extra delivered
$\dfrac{11}{100} = .11 = 11\%$ were over-shipped

8. $85 - 82 = \dfrac{3}{85} = .04 = 4\%$ missing

9. $\dfrac{35}{5,000} = .007 = .7\%$ damaged

10. $\dfrac{32}{50} = .64 = 64\%$ of single rooms booked
$\dfrac{89}{120} = .74 = 74\%$ of double rooms booked
$\dfrac{12}{30} = .40 = 40\%$ of suites booked
$32 + 89 + 12 = 133$
$200 - 133 = \dfrac{67}{200} = .335 = 33.5\%$ or 34% of the hotel was empty

11. $\dfrac{1}{8} = .125$
$\$740,000 \times .125 = \$92,500$ amount sales were down
$\$740,000 - \$92,500 = \$647,500$ amount of sales this year.

12. $\dfrac{\$\ 300}{\$1,500} = \dfrac{1}{5} = .2 = 20\%$ go to taxes

13. $\dfrac{32}{40,000} = .0008 = .08\%$ returned

14. $\dfrac{\$1,800}{\$1,200} = \dfrac{3}{2} = 1.50 = 150\%$

15. $\dfrac{56,000}{50,000} = 1.12 = 112\%$ of maximum capacity

16. $\dfrac{7}{3,500} = .0020 = .2\%$ flawed

    $15,000 \times .002$ 30 copies might be flawed.

17. $\dfrac{4}{880} = .0045 = .005 = .5\%$ Yes, she should call for service.

18. $\dfrac{\$8,350}{\$5,550} = 1.504 = 1.50 = 150\%$ of last year.

    Goal $(2 \times \$5,550) - \$8,350 = \$2,750.00$

19. $\dfrac{\$\ 8,062.50}{\$10,750.00} = .75$ or 75%

    $100\% - 75\% = 25\%$

20. $22 \times 10 = 220$
    $220 - 150 = 70$ miles further on each tank of gas
    $\dfrac{70}{150} = 47\%$ increase in distance

21. $210 \times 3\% = 210 \times .03 = 6.30$ rooms $= 6$ rooms
    210 rooms $- 6$ rooms $= 204$ rooms booked
    $204 \times 10\%$ no show rate $= 20$ rooms
    6 rooms $+ 20$ rooms $= 26$ rooms probably available

22. $2,452 \times \dfrac{3}{4} = 1,839$ signed up for insurance

    $1,839 \times .7 = 1,287$ selected an HMO

    $\dfrac{1,287}{2,452} = .524 = 52\%$ of the employees joined company sponsored HMOs

23. $\$33,500 \times 7\dfrac{1}{2}\% = \$33,500 \times .075 = \$2,512.50$

24. Supervisor $= \dfrac{\$12,525}{\$25,050} = .50 = 50\%$

    Jay's rate of commission is $\dfrac{1}{2}$ of 50% or 25%. $\$4,350 \times .25 = \$1,087.50$

CHAPTER 2 Percent Applications

LESSON 7 Finding Commissions   pages 31-33

EXERCISE 7

1. $980	2. $12,300	3. $68,600	4. $570
×.05	×.25	×.04	×.20
$49.00	61500	$2,744.00	$114.00
	+ 246000		
	$3,075.00		

Change the percent to a decimal and multiply the sales by the percent.

5. $63,900 × .03 = $1,917.00 Multiply the sales by the commission rate.

USE WHAT YOU HAVE LEARNED

1. $1400	2. $22,500	3. $13,400	4. $58,200
×.07	×.12	×.09	×.25
$98.00	45000	$1,206.00	291000
	+ 225000		+ 1164000
	$2,700.00		$14,550.00

Change the percent to a decimal and multiply the sales by the percent.

5. Multiply the premium amount by the commission rate: $1180 × .40 = $472.00.

6. The question asks you to multiply the amount of sales ($4,900) by the commission rate (25%): $4,900 × .25 = $1,225.

7. Multiply the sales by the commission rate: $144,000 × .04 = $5,760.

8. First find the total amount of sales by adding: $950 + $480 + $1,260 + $390 = $3,080. Then multiply that total ($3,080) by the commission rate (8%): $3,080 × .08 = $246.40.

9. Multiply the sales by the commission rate: $135,000 × .12 = $16,200.00. Then add this number to the salary: $16,200 + $15,000 = $31,200.

10. First subtract to find the amount of sales over $1,000: $2,700 − $1,000 = $1,700. Then multiply that amount by the commission rate: $1,700 × .16 = $272.00. Add that number to the salary: $272 + $150 = $422.

LESSON 8 Percent of Increase   **pages 34-37**

EXERCISE 8

1. .6 = 60%   80 − 50 = 30   30 ÷ 50 = .6

2. .375 = 37.5%   11 − 8 = 3   3 ÷ 8 = .375

3. $.4 = 40\% \quad 2{,}100 - 1{,}500 = 600 \quad 600 \div 1{,}500 = .4$

4. $.5 = 50\% \quad 9 - 6 = 3 \quad 3 \div 6 = .5$

Subtract the original value from the new value, divide the amount of increase by the original value, and change the decimal to a percent.

5. 5% Subtract the original pay from the new pay: $10.50 - 10.00 = \$ .50$. Then divide that amount by the original pay: $\$ .50 \div \$10 = .05 = 5\%$.

USE WHAT YOU HAVE LEARNED

1. $.3 = 30\% \quad 65 - 50 = 15 \quad 15 \div 50 = .3$

2. $.6 = 60\% \quad 32 - 20 = 12 \quad 12 \div 20 = .6$

3. $.25 = 25\% \quad 15 - 12 = 3 \quad 3 \div 12 = .25$

4. $.05 = 5\% \quad 42{,}000 - 40{,}000 = 2{,}000 \quad 2{,}000 \div 40{,}000 = .05$

Subtract the original value from the new value, divide the amount of increase by the original value, and change the decimal to a percent.

5. 40% Subtract the original number of employees from the new number: $70 - 50 = 20$. Then divide by the original number of employees: $20 \div 50 = .4$.

6. 14% Subtract the original pay per hour from the new pay: $4.41 - 6.50 = .91$. Then divide by the original pay: $.91 \div 6.50 = .14$.

7. 37.5% Subtract the original hours worked (from the new hours worked: $33 - 24 = 9$. Then divide by the original hours worked: $9 \div 24 = .375$

8. 72% Subtract the first quarter sales from the second quarter sales: $43{,}860 - 25{,}500 = 18{,}360$. Then divide by the first quarter sales: $18{,}360 \div 25{,}500 = .72$

9. The amount of increase is $27.54. The percent of increase is 8.5%. Subtract the original salary from the new salary: $351.54 - 324.00 = 27.54$. Then divide by the original salary: $27.54 \div 324 = .085 = 8.5\%$.

10. The amount of increase if $1,692. The percent of increase is 9%. Subtract the original salary from the new salary: $20{,}492 - 18{,}800 = 1{,}692$. Then divide by the original salary: $1{,}692 \div 18{,}800 = .09 = 9\ \%$.

LESSON 9 Percent of Decrease
pages 38-41

EXERCISE 9

1. $.2 = 20\% \quad 3.5 - 2.8 = .7 \quad .7 \div 3.5 = .2$

2. $.07 = 7\% \quad 8 - 7.44 = .56 \quad .56 \div 8 = .07$

3. $.175 = 17.5\% \quad 120 - 99 = 21 \quad 21 \div 120 = .175$

4. $.25 = 25\% \quad 72 - 54 = 18 \quad 18 \div 72 = .25$

Subtract the new value from the original value, divide the amount of decrease by the original value, and change the decimal to a percent.

5. 37.5% decrease Subtract the new number of employees from the original number of employees: $8 - 5 = 3$. Divide by the original number of employees: $3 \div 8 = .375$.

USE WHAT YOU HAVE LEARNED

1. $.2 = 20\%$ $50 - 40 = 10$ $10 \div 50 = .2$

2. $.1 = 10\%$ $250 - 225 = 25$ $25 \div 250 = .1$

3. $.125 = 12.5\%$ $12 - 10.5 = 1.5$ $1.5 \div 10.5 = .125$

4. $.11 = 11\%$ $32,500 - 28,925 = 3,575$ $3,575 \div 32,500 = .11$

Subtract the new value from the original value, divide the amount of decrease by the original value, and change the decimal to a percent.

5. 48% decrease Subtract the new sales amount from the original sales amount: $\$16,400 - \$8,528 = \$7,872$. Divide by the original amount: $\$7,872 \div \$16,400 = .48$.

6. 40% decrease Subtract the new time from the original time: $25 - 15 = 10$. Divide this by the original time: $10 \div 15 = .4$.

7. 15% decrease Subtract the new enrollment from the original enrollment: $60 - 51 = 9$. Divide by the original enrollment: $9 \div 60 = .15$.

8. 8% decrease Subtract the new temperature from the original temperature: $75 - 69 = 6$. Divide by the original enrollment: $6 \div 75 = .08$.

9. 60% decrease Subtract the new number ordered from the original number ordered: $20 - 8 = 12$. Divide by the original number ordered: $12 \div 20 = .6$.

10. 30% decrease Subtract the new price from the original price. Divide by the original price: $84 \div 280 = .3$.

LESSON 10 Pie Graphs and Bar Graphs   pages 42-46

EXERCISE 10A

1. Shift #2 produces 28% or $345,000 \times .28 = 96,600$ cars.

2. Shift #1 produces 13,800 more cars than Shift #3. $110,400 - 62,100 = 48,300$

3. Shifts 3 and #4 produce 138,000 cars.
   Shift #3 produces 18% or $345,000 \times .18 = 62,100$ cars
   Shift #4 produces 22% or $345,000 \times .22 = 75,900$ cars
   $62,100 + 75,900 = 138,000$

4. Shift #4 would have to produce 34,500 more cars. $110,400 - 75,900 = 34,500$

5. The first two shifts produced more cars.

Shift #1	110,400	Shift #3	62,100
Shift #2	+96,600	Shift #4	+75,900
	207,000		138,000

6. Jan	5%	**9.** Apr	9%	**12.** Jul	10%	**15.** Oct	7%
7. Feb	7%	**10.** May	10%	**13.** Aug	9%	**16.** Nov	9%
8. Mar	9%	**11.** Jun	10%	**14.** Sep	8%	**17.** Dec	7%

18. January had the lowest sales.

USE WHAT YOU HAVE LEARNED

1. $18,000 $150,000 × .12=$18,000

2. 8% This can be read directly from the graph.

3. $7,500 $150,000 × .05=$7,500

4. 2% This can be directly from the graph.

5. $30,000 This is the total cost of management. $150,000 × .2 = $30,000

6.
Management salaries	20%
Staff/wages	53%
Total spent on salaries and wages	73%

7.
Equipment maintenance	=	$12,000
Fuel	=	$ 7,500
Total Equipment and Fuel	=	$19,500

8. Shift #1 qualified for the bonus because 110,400 > 95,000.
Shift #2 qualified for the bonus because 96,600 > 95,000.
2 shifts × 1,000 workers × $100 each= $200,000 paid in bonuses

9. 20,540 days were missed by workers on Shift #3.
1,000 workers × 260 days × 7.9% absenteeism rate = 1,000 × 260 × .079

10. The Second Quarter had the highest sales.

Jan	$12,550	Apr	$23,000	Jul	$26,000	Oct	$18,500
Feb	$18,250	May	$24,500	Aug	$22,000	Nov	$22,100
Mar	+$22,250	Jun	+$25,000	Sep	+$19,350	Dec	+$16,500
	$53,050		$72,500		$67,350		$57,100

11. The lowest sales month, "Jan," did occur in the lowest sales quarter, the First Quarter. The highest sales month, "Jul," **did not** occur in the highest sales quarter, the Second Quarter.

LESSON 11 Using Information from Graphs   pages 47-50

1. 1992   1991 saw 600 flights, 1992 saw 500.

2. Flights in 1992 were 71% of flights in 1993. $\frac{500}{700}$ = .714285, or 71%

3. 1993 saw the largest percent of increase. $700 - 500 = 200$

$\frac{200}{500} = .4 \times 100 = 40\%$ 1994-95 also saw an increase of 200 flights, but the

percent of increase was smaller. $1{,}000 - 800 = 200$ $\frac{200}{800} = .25$, or 25%

4. There was a decrease in total spending between 1991 and 1995.

1991=\$50 million   1995=\$40 million   \$50 million > \$40 million

5. \$30 million 40% of spending went to environmental protection.
$75{,}000{,}000 \times .4 = \$30{,}000{,}000$

6. \$20 million was the total increase in spending between 1991 and 1993.
\$70 million − \$50 million = \$20 million

7. 60% In 1994, 20% of \$75 million, or \$15 million, was spent on economic
development. $75{,}000{,}000 \times .2 = 15{,}000{,}000$

In 1995, 60% of \$40 million, or \$24 million, was spent on economic
development. $40{,}000{,}000 \times .6 = \$24{,}000{,}000$

The percent of increase is 60%. $24{,}000{,}000 - 15{,}000{,}000 = 9{,}000{,}000$
$9{,}000{,}000 \div 15{,}000{,}000 = .6$

8. The percent spending in environmental protection remained the same in
1991-92 and in 1993-94.

1991 and 1992 = 30% spending in Environmental Protection

1993 and 1994 = 40% spending in Environmental Protection

USE WHAT YOU HAVE LEARNED

1. % of decrease = 73%

$$\frac{(.4 \times \$75) - (.2 \times \$40)}{(.4 \times \$75)} = \frac{30 - 8}{30} = \frac{22}{30} = .73$$

33,215 jobs would be cut. 73% of 45,500 jobs = $.73 \times 45{,}500 = 33{,}215$

2. The percent decrease in spending on Environmental Protection between 1992
and 1993 was 36%.

1992 = 40% of \$55 million   1993 = 20% of \$70 million

$\quad$ = $.4 \times \$55$ million $\quad$ = $.2 \times \$70$ million

$\quad\quad$ = \$22 million $\quad\quad$ = \$14 million

The percent of decrease = 36%

$$\frac{\$22 \text{ mil} - \$14 \text{ mil}}{\$22 \text{ mil}}$$

$$= \frac{\$8 \text{ mil}}{\$22 \text{ mil}}$$

$$= \frac{4}{11} = .36$$

3. The average amount spent in Health, Education and Welfare during the five year period shown on the graph is $19,500,000.

$$1991 = 30\% \text{ of } \$50 \text{ mil} = .3 \times 50 = \$15 \text{ mil}$$
$$1992 = 30\% \text{ of } \$55 \text{ mil} = .3 \times 55 = \$16.5 \text{ mil}$$
$$1993 = 40\% \text{ of } \$70 \text{ mil} = .4 \times 70 = \$28 \text{ mil}$$
$$1994 = 40\% \text{ of } \$75 \text{ mil} = .4 \times 75 = \$30 \text{ mil}$$
$$1995 = 20\% \text{ of } \$40 \text{ mil} = .2 \, 3 \, 40 = \underline{\$+8 \text{ mil}}$$

Total spent $\qquad \$97.5 \text{ mil}$

$$\text{Average} = \frac{97.5}{5} = 19.5 \text{ or } \$19,500,000$$

4. More money was spent on Economic Development in 1995.

$$1994 = 20\% \text{ of } \$75 \text{ mil} = .2 \times 75 = \$15 \text{ mil}$$
$$1995 = 60\% \text{ of } \$40 \text{ mil} = .6 \times 40 = \$24 \text{ mil}$$

CHAPTER 2 Summary pages 51-52

EXERCISE A

1. $282 $1,880 \times .15 = 282$

2. $1,356 $11,300 \times .12 = 1,356$

3. $4,341.60 $72,360 \times .06 = 4,341.6$

4. $167 $835 \times .2 = 167$

If you have trouble, refer to Lesson 7.

EXERCISE B

Find the percent of increase.

5. 37.5% or 38% $65 - 40 = 15 \div 40 = .375$

6. 33.3% or 33% $8 - 6 = 2 \div 6 = .333$

7. 83.3% or 83% $2,200 - 1,200 = 1,000 \div 1,200 = .833$

8. 30% $26,000 - 20,000 = 6,000 \div 20,000 = .3$

If you have trouble, refer to Lesson 8.

EXERCISE C

9. 25% $36 - 27 = 9 \quad 9 \div 36 = .25$

10. 16.6% or 17% $150 - 125 = 25 \quad 25 \div 150 = .166$

11. 5% $10 - 9.5 = .5 \quad .5 \div 10 = .05$

12. 31.25% or 31% $32,000 - 22,000 = 10,000 \quad 10,000 \div 32,000 = .3125$

If you have trouble, refer to Lesson 9.

13. 63% is represented by take-home pay. $100 - (15 + 10 + 12) = 100 - 37 = 63$

14. $69,600 were paid for Social Security last year. $464,000 \times .15 = 69,600$

15. $125,280 were paid in Social Security and Income Tax. $464,000 \times .12 = 55,680$
$464,000 \times .15 = 69,600$ $55,680 + 69,600 = 125,280$

If you have trouble, refer to Lessons 10 and 11.

CHAPTER 2   Math at Work   pages 53-56

1. John's commission was $23,565. 30% of $78,550 = $.3 \times \$78,550 = \$23,565$
Boyd's commission was $33,000. 40% of $82,500 = $.4 \times \$82,500 = \$33,000$

2. The number of employees increased by 43%. $\dfrac{33 - 23}{23} = \dfrac{10}{23} = .43 \text{ or } 43\%$

3. Sales decreased by 21%. $\dfrac{\$35,000 - \$27,500}{\$35,000} = \dfrac{\$7,500}{\$35,000} = .21 = 21\%$

4. Anna's total commission was $2,550.
$4,900 at 25% $4,900 \times .25 = \qquad \$1,225$

$5,300 at 25% $5,300 \times .25 = \dfrac{+\$1,325}{\$2,550}$

5. Ella's pay increased 11%. $\dfrac{\$7.00 - \$6.25}{\$7.00} = \dfrac{\$.75}{\$7.00} = .11 = 11\%$

6. The time needed decreased 35%.
$\dfrac{6 \text{ min } 30 \text{ sec} - 4 \text{ min } 15 \text{ sec}}{6 \text{ min } 30 \text{ sec}} = \dfrac{6.5 \text{ min} - 4.25 \text{ min}}{6.5 \text{ min}} = \dfrac{2.25}{6.50} = .35 = 35\%$

7. Pete's commission was $10,525. $210,500 \times 5\% = \$210,500 \times .05 = \$10,525.00$

8. Arnold earned $54 more this month than last month.
Last month: $6.50 \times 24 = \$156$
This month: $7.00 \times 30 = \$210$

Arnold's pay increased 26%.
$\dfrac{\$210 - 156}{\$210} = \dfrac{\$54}{\$210} = .26 = 26\% \text{ increase}$

9. Truancy decreased by 23%. $\dfrac{4,035 - 3,123}{4,035} = \dfrac{912}{4.035} = .23 = 23\%$

10. Norma's total commission was $851.
8% of ($950 + $1,250) $.08 \times \$2,200 = \qquad \$ 176$

10% of ($2,250 + $4,500) $.10 \times \$6,750 = \dfrac{+\$ 675}{\$851}$

Total Commission for the week

11. $40,700 is gained through telemarketing.

$100\% - (28\% + 35\%) = 37\%$ due to telemarketing

$.37 \times \$110,000 = \$40,700$

12. Randy's average monthly salary is $4,000

$\$1,650,000 \times 2\% = \$1,650,000 \times 0.02 = \$33,000$

$\$33,000 + \$15,000 = \$48,000$

$\$48,000 \div 12 = \$4,000$

13. Circulation has increased by 18%. $\dfrac{12,550-10,245}{12,550} = \dfrac{2,305}{12,550} = .18 = 18\%$

14. The sales at Great Buys were 162% of those at the department store.

Great Buys: 56 food processors at $129.95 each

$56 \times \$129.95 = \$7,277.20$

Department Store: 28 food processors at $159.95 each

$28 \times \$19.95 = \$4.478.60$

Great Buys: $\dfrac{\$7,277.20}{\$4,478.60} = 1.6248827$ or 162%
Department Store:

15. Marta's percent of increase in sales calls did not equal her percent of increase in sales.

Sales calls: $\dfrac{56 - 25}{25} = \dfrac{31}{25} = 1.24 = 124\%$

Sales: $\dfrac{\$3,650 - \$2,700}{\$2.700} = \dfrac{\$\,950}{2,700} = .35 = 35\%$

16. Jack made $50,200 more than Frank.

Jack: $1 \times \$1.3$ million $\times 10\% = \$1,300,000 \times .10 = \$130,000$

Frank: $7 \times \$95,000 \times 12\% = 7 \times \$95,000 \times .12 = \$79,800$

17. Jack's commission was 63% more than Frank's commission.

Jack's commission	$130,000	$\dfrac{\$50,200}{\$79,800} = .6290726$, or 63%
Frank's commission	$-\$79,800	
difference	$50,200	

18. Mel's secretary earned $261 in commission.

$14 \times \$90 \times 7\% = \$1,260 \times .07 = \$88.20$

$12 \times \$180 \times 8\% = \$2,160 \times .08 = \$172.80$

$\$172,8 + \$88.20 = \$261.00$

19. The difference in total sales is $44,100.

$\$245,000 \times 38\% = \$245,00 \times .38 = \$93,100$

$\$245,000 \times 20\% = \$245,00 \times .2 = \$49,000$

$93,100 - \$49,000 = \$44,100.$

20. Anne's profit is $316.25.

$\$1,265 \times 25\% = \$1,265 \times .25 = \$316.25$

21. Her total commission is $703.75.

$\$1,555 \times 25\% = \$1,555 \times .25 = \$388.75$

$\$750 \times 42\% = \$750 \times .42 = \$315.00$

$\$388.75 + \$315.00 = \$703.75$

22. Foreign-made car sales decreased 17%.

$$\frac{5,255 - 4,355}{5,255} = \frac{900}{5,255} = .17 = 17\%$$

Domestic car sales increased 62%.

$$\frac{5,655 - 3,490}{3,490} = \frac{2,165}{3,490} = .62 = 62\%$$

23. Alex's total earnings for the month will be $2,173.50.
$1,245 \times 30\% = \$1,245 \times .30 = \$373.50$
$1,800 + \$373.50 = \$2,173.50$

CHAPTER 3 The Part, the Whole, the Percent

LESSON 12 Finding Part of a Number   pages 57-59

EXERCISE 12

1.
```
    45
×  .19
   405
+ 450
  8.55
```

2.
```
   178
×  .05
   890
+ 000
  8.90
```

3.
```
   1.25
×  $51
   125
+ 6250
$63.75
```

4.
```
  $296.99
×     .33
    89097
+ 890970
$98.0067    $98.01
```

5.
```
    95
×   .4
  38.0
```

6.
```
    169
×  .375
    845
  11830
+ 50700
 63.375
```

7.
```
  47.25
×   .75
  23625
+ 330750
 35.4375    $35.44
```

8.
```
  $172
×   .2
 $34.4
```

Did you convert the percent to a decimal? Did you move the decimal to the left two places in the product? If your answer is in dollars, did you round to the nearest hundredth?

9. $2.60   The question asks you to determine the savings when a $12.99 CD is 20% off. $12.99 × .20 = $2.598

1.
$$50 \times .12$$
100
+ 50
6.00   6

2.
$$286 \times 1.17$$
2002
2860
+ 28600
334.62

3.
$$50 \times .65$$
250
+ 3000
32.50   32.5

4.
$$1{,}880 \times .18$$
15040
+ 18800
338.40   338.4

5.
$$75 \times .15$$
375
+750
11.25

6.
$$1.36 \times 121$$
136
2720
+ 13600
164.56

7.
$$.25 \times 50$$
12.50   12.5

8.
$$86 \times .003$$
.258

Did you convert the percent to a decimal? Did you move the decimal to the left two places in the product? If your answer is in dollars, did you round to the nearest hundredth?

9. 24 employees are full time. The question asks you to determine the number representing 80% of the 30 employees.

10. Sandy has 9 children 2 years old or younger. The question asks you to determine 30% of 30 children.

11. The savings on the television are $134.40. The question asks you to determine 15% of the price of an $895.99 television.

12. Paul will hire 10 employees. He will then have 18 people working for him. This is a multi-step problem. Rename 125% as 1.25. To find how many people Paul will hire to reach his goal, multiply the decimal (1.25) by the number of employees working for Paul now: $1.25 \times 8 = 10.00$. To find how many employees Paul will have if he reaches his goal, add the number of people working for him now (8) with the number he wants to hire (10): $8 + 10 = 18$.

13. 153 listeners are not between the ages of seventeen and twenty-nine. This is a multi-step problem. To find the number of listeners between the ages of seventeen and twenty-nine, change the number of people polled (408) into a fraction and multiply it by the fraction of listeners between the ages of seventeen and twenty-nine ($\frac{5}{8}$): $\frac{408}{1} \times \frac{5}{8} = \frac{2040}{8}$. Rename the fraction as a proper fraction by dividing the numerator by the denominator: $2{,}040 \div 8 = 255$. To find how many people are not between the specified ages, subtract the listeners between the ages of seventeen and twenty-nine (255) from the total number of people polled (408): $408 - 255 = 153$.

14. The customer will save $7. The blouse will cost $21. Including tax, the blouse will cost $22.58. This is a multi-step problem. To find how much the customer will save, multiply the fraction off ($\frac{1}{4}$) by the price of the blouse($28): $\frac{1}{4} \times \frac{$28}{1}$ = $\frac{$28}{4}$ or $7. To find how much the blouse will cost with the discount, subtract the savings ($7) from the total cost of the blouse ($28): $28− $7= $21. Rename the 7.5 tax percent as the decimal .075. To find the tax charge, multiply the tax rate (.075) by the cost of the blouse ($21): $21 × .075 = $1.575 or $1.58. To find the cost of the blouse, add the cost of the blouse ($21) with the tax ($1.58): $21.00 + $1.58 = $22.58.

15. Isako saves $28.95 each month and $347.40 each year. This is a multi-step problem. Rename the percent as a decimal: 5% = .05. To find how much Isako saves each week, multiply the amount she earns ($578.93) by the decimal of the percent: $578.93 × .05 = $28.946 or $28.95. To find how much Isako saves in one year, multiply the monthly savings ($28.95) by the number of months in one year (12): $28.95 × 12 = $347.40.

LESSON 13 Finding a Number From its Percent   pages 60-62

EXERCISE 13 ──

1. 76 25% = .25   19 ÷ .25 = 1,900 ÷ 25 = 76

2. 869.62 79% = .79   687 ÷ .79 = 68,700 ÷ 79 = 869.620

3. $2,134 2% =.02 $42.68 ÷ .02 = $4,268 ÷ 2 = $2,134

4. 2,156.25 16% = .16   345 ÷ .16 = 34,500 ÷ 16 = 2,156.25

Convert the percent to a decimal and divide the part by the percent.

5. 730 wafers were ordered Determine the total number processed if 60%, or 438 wafers, have already been processed. 438 ÷ .6 = 730

USE WHAT YOU HAVE LEARNED ──────────────────────────

1. 280 15% = .15   42 ÷ .15 = 4,200 ÷ 15 = 280

2. 80 70% = .7   56 ÷ .7 = 560 ÷ 7 = 80

3. 626.25 80% = .8   501 ÷ .8 = 5,010 ÷ 8 = 626.25

4. 180 35% = .35   66 ÷ .35 = 6,300 ÷ 35 = 180

5. 280 10% = .1   28 ÷ .1 = 280 ÷ 1 = 280

6. 328 3% = .03   9.84 ÷ .03 = 984 ÷ 3 = 328

7. $36 21% = .21 $7.56 ÷ .21 = $756 ÷ 21 = $36

8. $1,448 64% = .64 $926.72 ÷ .64 = $92,672 ÷ 64 = $1,448

Convert the percent to a decimal and divide the part by the percent.

9. **7.5 total hours worked** The question asks you to determine the total number of hours worked if 40% of the day, or 3 hours, is spent delivering mail. $3 \div .4 = 7.5$

10. **160 vehicles on the lot** The question asks you to determine the total number of vehicles if 45%, or 72 trucks, are on the lot. $72 \div .45 = 160$

11. **468 boxes** The question asks you to determine the total number of boxes to be delivered if 25%, or 117 boxes, are loaded onto a truck. $117 \div .25 = 468$

12. **$87,000 is the total price.** Determine the total price of a house if 33% is $28,710: $28,710 \div .33 = \$87,000$.

13. **Zack is short 100 feet of lights. He will need 1 more box of lights.** This is a multi-step problem. To find the total feet of lights, multiply the number of boxes (4) by the number of feet in each box (100): $4 \times 100 = 400$. To find the total distance around the deck, divide the number of feet of lights Zack has (400) by the percent of the deck the lights cover (80% or .8): $400 \div .8 = 500$. To find how many boxes short Zack is, divide the total number of feet he needs (100) by the number of feet in a box of lights (100): $100 \div 100 = 1$.

14. **The rings cost $179, and the store had 120 to sell.** This problem is a multi-step problem. To find how much the rings originally cost, divide the selling price ($89.50) by the percent of the sale (50% or .5): $89.50 \div .5 = \$179$. To find the total number of rings the store had in stock to sell, divide the number of rings sold (108) by the percent sold (90% or .9): $108 \div .9 = 120$.

LESSON 14 **Finding the Original Price** pages 63-65

EXERCISE 14

1. **$20** $100\% - 20\% = 80\%$ $80\% = .8$ $\$16 \div .8 = \$160 \div 8 = \$20$

2. **$15** $100\% - 70\% = 30\%$ $30\% = .3$ $\$4.50 \div .3 = \$45 \div 3 = \$15$

3. **$60** $100\% - 25\% = 75\%$ $75\% = .75$ $\$45 \div .75 = \$4,500 \div 75 = \$60$

4. **$824** $100\% - 75\% = 25\%$ $25\% = .25$ $\$206 \div .25 = \$20,600 \div 25 = \$824$

   Subtract to find the percent difference, convert the percent to a decima, and divide the discounted price by the decimal form of the percent difference.

5. **$40.55 is the original cost of the sweater.** The question asks you to determine the original cost of a sweater that is on sale for $24.33 and has been reduced 40%. $100\% - 40\% = 60\%$ or .6 $\$243.3 \div 6 = \$40.55$

USE WHAT YOU HAVE LEARNED

1. **$4** $100\% - 5\% = 95\%$ $95\% = .95$ $\$3.80 \div .95 = \$380 \div 95 = \$4$

2. **$140** $100\% - 30\% = 70\%$ $70\% = .7$ $\$98 \div .7 = \$980 \div 7 = \$140$

3. **$168** $75\% - 25\% = 25\%$ $25\% = .25$ $\$42 \div .25 = \$4,200 \div 25 = \$824$

4. **$325** $100\% - 20\% = 80\%$ $80\% = .8$ $\$260 \div .8 = \$2,600 \div 8 = \$325$

5. **$300** $100\% - 67\% = 33\%$ $33\% = .33$ $\$99 \div .33 = \$9,900 \div 33 = \$300$

6. $32.50 $100\% - 40\% = 60\%$ $60\% = .6$ $\$19.50 \div .6 = \$195 \div 6 = \$32.50$

7. $72.50 $100\% - 20\% = 80\%$ $80\% = .8$ $\$58 \div .8 = \$580 \div 8 = \$72.50$

8. $20 $100\% - 24\% = 66\%$ $66\% = .66$ $\$13.20 \div .66 = \$1,320 \div 66 = \$20$

Subtract to find the percent difference, convert the percent to a decimal, and divide the discounted price by the decimal form of the percent.

9. $700 is the original cost of the fax. The question asks you to determine the original price when Doug pays $525 for a fax machine discounted 25%.
$100\% - 25\% = 75\%$ or $.75$ $\$52,500 \div 75 = \$700$

10. $911.25 is the original cost of the lease. Determine the price after one year when Eric leases an office for $729 per month discounted 20%.
$100\% - 20\% = 80\%$ or $.8$ $\$7,290 \div 8 = \$911.25$

11. $80 was the riginal cost of the brief case. The question asks you to determine the original price when Marilyn pays $52.80 for a brief case discounted 34%.
$100\% - 34\% = 66\%$ or $.66$ $\$5,280 \div 66 = \$80$

12. $594 is the full price of the saddle. The question asks you to determine the retail price when the wholesale price ($297) is 50% of the retail price.
$100\% - 50\% = 50\%$ or $.5$ $\$2,970 \div 5 = \$594.$

13. The original cost of the shirt is $6. If Fran orders 20 shirts, she will pay $5.40 per shirt. If she orders 20 shirts, she will save 30¢ on each shirt. This is a multi-step problem. To find the original cost of the shirts, divide the discounted price ($5.70) by the decimal form of the percent difference (95% or .95): $\$5.70 \div .95 = \$6$. To find the price of each shirt if twenty are ordered, multiply the original shirt cost ($6) by the difference in the decimal form of the percent (90% or .9): $\$6 \times .9 = \$5.40$. To find the savings per shirt, subtract the price of the 10% discounted shirt ($5.40) from the 5% discounted shirt ($5.70): $\$5.70 - \$5.40 = .30$.

14. The original price of each dinner is $9.40. The total savings on the dinners with the discount will be $169.20. This is a multi-step problem. To find the price Sandra usually charges per steak dinner, divide the discounted price ($7.99) by the difference in the decimal form of the percent difference (85% or .85): $\$7.99 \div .85 = \$9.40$. To find the total savings, first find the cost of 120 dinners at the discounted price of $7.99: $120 \times \$7.99 = \$958.80$. Then find the cost of 120 dinners at the original price of $9.40: $120 \times \$9.40 = \$1,128.00$. Find the difference in the two: $\$1,128.00 - \$958.80 = \$169.20$.

LESSON 15 Finding Percent From the Part and Whole   pages 66-68

EXERCISE 15

1. 25% $9 \div 36 = .25$ 2. 40% $26 \div 65 = .4$ 3. 12.5% or 13% $12 \div 96 = .125$

Divide the part by the whole and convert the decimal to a percent.

4. 13% of the boxes are unpacked. Determine the percent when 13 of 100 boxes are unpacked. $13.00 \div 100 = .13$

1. 1% .09 ÷ 9 = .01   2. 67% or 66.6% 12 ÷ 18 = .66   3. 6% 9 ÷ 54 = .06

4. 40% 4 ÷ 10 = .4   5. 70% 56 ÷ 80 = .7   6. 75% 48 ÷ 64 = .75

Divide the part by the whole and convert the decimal to a percent.

7. 68% have given blood. The question asks you to determine percent of employees who have donated blood when 85 of 125 have already done so. 85 ÷ 125 = .68 or 68%

8. The book is reduced 38%. The question asks you to determine percent of reduction when a $4.80 book is reduced to $3.00. $480 − $3.00 = $1.80 $180 ÷ $4.80 = .375 or 38%

9. 25% of the children at the day care are four year olds. This is a multi-step problem. To find the number of 4 year olds, multiply the number of students (9) by the number of classes (2): 9 × 2 = 18. To find the percent of four year olds at the day care are, divide the part of four year olds (18) by the whole number of students (72): 18 ÷ 72 = .25 or 25%.

10. Ada paid a 13% deposit and will make a $142 dollar payment each month for 6 months. This is a multi-step problem. To find the percent of deposit, subtract the amount left to pay ($852) from the total ($980): $980 − $852 = $128. Divide the part of the deposit paid ($128) by the whole amount ($980): $128 ÷ $980 = .13 or 13%. To find the 6 equal payments, divide the amount left to pay ($852) by the number of months (6): $852 ÷ 6 = $142.

11. Pete has a 15% discount card and pays $19.89 for his dinner using the discount card. This is a multi-step problem. To find the percent of the card, subtract the amount Pete pays for the hotel ($68) from the total ($80): $80 − $68 = $12. Divide the difference ($12) by the whole amount of the hotel ($80): $12 ÷ $80 = .15 or 15%. To find how much discount Pete gets on dinner, multiply the total price ($23.40) by the percent difference of the card in decimal form: $23.40 × .85 = $19.89.

12. Don has visited 22% of the stores and has 74% of the miles to go. This is a multi-step problem. To find the percent of stores visited, divide the number of stores visited (2) by the total number of stores (9): 2 ÷ 9 = .222 or 22%. To find the percent of miles left to travel, subtract the miles traveled (403) from the total miles (1,550): 1,550 − 403 = 1,147. Divide the difference (1,147) by the total miles (1,550): 1,147 ÷ 1,550 = .74 or 74%.

LESSON 16 Applying Proportion to Percent Problems   pages 69-72

EXERCISE 16

1. $\frac{5}{25} = \frac{20}{100}$ 2. $\frac{48}{64} = \frac{75}{100}$ 3. $\frac{399.84}{588} = \frac{68}{100}$

4. $\dfrac{45}{112.5} = \dfrac{40}{100}$ **5.** $\dfrac{450}{250} = \dfrac{180}{100}$ **6.** $\dfrac{306.24}{348} = \dfrac{88}{100}$

Cross multiply the diagonal pair of numbers, and then divide by the remaining number.

7. Her whole trip is 1,087 miles. $\dfrac{652}{?} = \dfrac{60}{100}$

$\dfrac{60}{100}$ reduces to $\dfrac{3}{5}$. Cross-multiply: $652 \times 5 = 3260$. Divide: $3260 \div 3 = 1{,}086.66$, or 1,087 miles.

USE WHAT YOU HAVE LEARNED

1. $\dfrac{44}{176} = \dfrac{25}{100}$ **2.** $\dfrac{64}{80} = \dfrac{80}{100}$ **3.** $\dfrac{240}{600} = \dfrac{40}{100}$

4. $\dfrac{38}{200} = \dfrac{19}{100}$ **5.** $\dfrac{225}{125} = \dfrac{180}{100}$ **6.** $\dfrac{13.632}{96} = \dfrac{14.2}{100}$

Cross multiply the diagonal pair of numbers, and then divide by the remaining number.

7. 20% still haven't taken the tour. $\dfrac{76}{95} = \dfrac{80}{100}$

$\dfrac{76}{95}$ reduces to $\dfrac{4}{5}$. Cross-multiply: $4 \times 100 = 400$. Divide: $400 \div 5 = 80$.

Subtract: $100 - 80 = 20$.

8. 176 eggs were required to hatch 22 turtles. $\dfrac{22}{176} = \dfrac{12.5}{100}$

Cross-multiply: $22 \times 100 = 2{,}200$. Divide: $2{,}200 \div 12.5 = 176$.

9. \$14.99 is what Max pays. $\dfrac{1.666}{16.66} = \dfrac{10}{100}$

Cross-multiply: $16.66 \times 10 = 166.6$. Divide: $166.6 \div 100 = 1.666$, or \$1.67.
Subtract: \$16.66 - \$1.67 = \$14.99.

10. 476 students will eat school lunch. 119 will eat fish sticks. $\dfrac{357}{476} = \dfrac{75}{100}$

$\dfrac{75}{100}$ reduces to $\dfrac{3}{4}$. Cross-multiply: $357 \times 4 = 1{,}428$. Divide: $1{,}428 \div 3 = 476$.

Subtract: $476 - 357 = 119$.

11. 86 % of Rita's T-shirt order has been completed. $\dfrac{120}{140} = \dfrac{85.71428}{100}$

$\dfrac{120}{140}$ reduces to $\dfrac{6}{7}$. Cross-multiply: $6 \times 100 = 600$. Divide: $600 \div 7 = 85.71428$, or 86%.

12. 50 yards is the distance around the room. No, Beverly does not have enough border to finish. 7.5 yards is the additional amount she needs.

$$\frac{12.5}{50} = \frac{25}{100}$$

2.5 yards $\times$ 2 = 12.5 yards. $\frac{25}{100}$ reduces to $\frac{1}{4}$. Multiply: 12.5 $\times$ 4 = 50.

Divide: 50 ÷ 1 = 50. 50 yards − 12.5 completed = 37.5 yards remaining. 6

rolls $\times$ 5 yards = 30 yards. 37.5 yards needed − 30 yards on hand = 7.5

yards needed.

CHAPTER 3 Summary pages 73-74

EXERCISE A

1. 9 is 15% of 60 60 $\times$ .15 = 9

2. 250 is 125% of 200 200 $\times$ 1.25 = 250

3. 40.5 is 45% of 90 90 $\times$ .45 = 40.5

If you have trouble, refer to Lesson 12.

EXERCISE B

4. 112 28 is 25% of 112 28 ÷ .25 = 112

5. 150 45 is 30% of 150 45 ÷ .3 = 150

6. 388.75 311 is 80% of 388.75 311 ÷ .8 = 388.75

7. 74 44.4 is 60% of 74 44.4 ÷ .6 = 74

If you have trouble, refer to Lesson 13.

EXERCISE C

8. $30.00 100% − 30% = 70%   21 ÷ .7 = 30

9. $14.03 100% − 60% = 40%   5.61 ÷ .4 = 14.025

10. $46.67 100% − 25% = 75%   35 ÷ .75 = 46.666

11. $588.89 100% − 64% = 36%   212 ÷ .64 = 588.888

If you have trouble, refer to Lesson 14.

EXERCISE D

12. 12.5% 8 of 64 is 12.5 percent 8 ÷ 64 = .125 $\times$ 100 = 12.5

13. 25% 6 of 24 is 25 percent 6 ÷ 24 = .25 $\times$ 100 = 25

14. 7.5% 48 of 640 is 7.5 percent 48 ÷ 640 = .075 $\times$ 100 = 7.5

15. 37.5% 27 of 72 is 37.5 percent 27 ÷ 72 = .375 $\times$ 100 = 37.5

If you have trouble, refer to Lesson 15.

16. $80 \quad \dfrac{24}{80} = \dfrac{30}{100} \qquad \dfrac{30}{100} = \dfrac{3}{10} \qquad 24 \times 10 = 240 \div 3 = 80$

17. $125\% \quad \dfrac{120}{96} = \dfrac{125}{100} \qquad \dfrac{120}{96} = \dfrac{5}{4} \qquad 5 \times 100 = 500 \div 4 = 125$

18. $120 \quad \dfrac{120}{400} = \dfrac{30}{100} \qquad \dfrac{30}{100} = \dfrac{3}{10} \qquad 400 \times 3 = 1200 \div 10 = 120$

If you have trouble, refer to Lesson 16.

CHAPTER 3 Math at Work   pages 75-78

1. $15,792.24 The question asks you to determine the amount of 3% from a $526,407 budget. $526,408 × .03 = $15,792.24

2. 128 rooms The question asks you to determine the total number of rooms at a hotel with 75% occupancy if 96 of the rooms are booked. 96 ÷ .75 = 128

3. $108.00 The question asks you to determine the original price of a frame when a customer pays $64.80 and uses a 40% discount. $64.80 ÷ .6 = $108.00

4. $5.96 The question asks you to determine the amount of savings on merchandise that costs $59.60 and is purchased with a 10% discount. $59.60 × .1 = $5.96

5. $1,204.96 The question asks you to determine the take-home salary from $1,807.44 when $\frac{1}{3}$ is taken out for benefits and taxes. $1,807.44 × $\frac{2}{3}$ = $1,204.96

6. 12.5% or 13% The question asks you to determine the percent of discount on an armoire that originally costs $1,600 and is marked down to $1,400. $1,600 − $1,400 = $200 $200 ÷ $1,600 = .125

7. 10 employees The question asks you to determine the total number of employees when 8, or 80%, are full time. 8 ÷ .8 = 10

8. 288.6 miles The question asks you to determine the how many miles 60% is of a total 481 miles. 480 × .6 = 288.6

9. $1,245 The question asks you to determine how much more Renee needs sell when she has sold $498, or 40%, of her whole goal. $498 ÷ .4 = $1,245

10. 150 classes The question asks you to determine the total number of classes offered when Lily teaches 27, or 18%, of all the classes. 27 ÷ .18 = 150

11. $80 The question asks you to determine the original price of a lamp when a customer pays $56 and the lamp was marked down 30%. $56 ÷ .7 = $80

12. The board is 8 feet long. Ed can cut 3 more boards. This is a multi-step problem. To find the length of the board, divide the amount cut from the board (2 feet) by the part cut off (25%): 2 ÷ .25 = 8. To find how many more 2 foot cuts can be made, subtract the amount already cut (2 feet) from the length (8 feet): 8 − 2 = 6. Then divide the length left (6 feet) by the length of the cuts (2 feet): 6 ÷ 2 = 3.

13. 44% of the pizzas being delivered are pepperoni. This is a multi-step problem. To find the total number of pizzas, add all the pizzas being delivered together: $1 + 2 + 2 + 4 = 9$. To find the percent of pepperoni pizzas, divide the number of pepperoni pizzas (4) by the total number (9): $4 \div 9 = .44$ or 44%.

14. Nathan had 625 flyers to deliver in all. This is a multi-step problem. To find the number of flyers that need to be delivered, multiply the number of packages (2) by the number in the packages (250): $2 \times 250 = 500$. To find the number of flyers Nathan began with, divide the amount left (500) by the percent of flyers given out (80%): $500 \div .8 = 625$.

15. $138.60 is saved The question asks you to determine the amount of savings when a $308 ticket is discounted 45%. $308 \times .45 = \$138.60$

16. The cost of the supplies will be $54.60 and the total cost with the dog will be $124.40. This is a multi-step problem. To find the price of the supplies with the discount, multiply the whole cost ($68.25) by the difference in the percent discount from 100% (80% or .8): $\$68.25 \times .8 = \$54.60$. Add the discounted price ($54.60) with the price of the dog ($69.80): $\$54.60 + \$69.80 = \$124.40$.

17. 36 classes The question asks you to determine the number of classes Laura needs to photograph when she has completed 27, or 75%, of them. $27 \div .75 = 36$

18. $81.00 The question asks you to determine the original price of cleaning supplies when a Belva pays $72.90 and gets a 10% cash discount. $\$72.90 \div .8 = \$81.00$

19. 37.5% or 38 % is left The question asks you to determine the percent of a 32 foot wall left to build when 20 feet has been done. $32 - 20 = 12 \quad 12 \div 32 = .375$

20. 57.5% or 58% of the rooms The question asks you to determine the percent of 160 rooms painted when 92 are done. $92 \div 160 = .575$

21. 23.9% or 24% discount The question asks you to determine the percent of discount when given the whole price and the marked down price. $\$52.50 - \$39.97 = \$12.53 \qquad \$1,253 \div \$5250 = .23866$

22. The curtains will take 75% of the fabric. This is a multi-step problem. to find the number of yards of fabric that will be used to make curtains, multiply the yards per set (9) by the number of sets to be sewn (2): $9 \times 2 = 18$. To find the percent of fabric to make curtains, divide the yardage for the curtains (18) by the number of total yards of fabric (24): $18 \div 24 = .75$ or 75%.

23. Andrew will interview 3 applicants. This is a multi-step problem. To find the number of qualified applicants, multiply the number of applicants (30) by the percent of qualified applicants (20% or .2): $30 \times .2 = 6$. To find the number of applicants Andrew will interview, divide the qualified applicants (6) by the fraction to interview $\left(\frac{1}{2}\right)$: $6 \div \frac{1}{2} = 3$.

24. $132 savings The question asks you to determine the savings when a $330 full-fare ticket is discounted 40%. $\$330 \times .4 = \$132.0$

CHAPTER 4 Interest

LESSON 17 The Meaning of Simple Interest   pages 79-82

EXERCISE 17A ――――――――――――――――――――――――――――――――

1. $35 $700 × .05 = $35.00 $35 × 1 = $35

2. $300 $5,000 × .06 = $300.00 $300 × 1 = $300

3. $54 $450 × .12 = $54.00 $54 × 1 = $54

4. $117 $1,300 × .09 = $117.00 $117 × 1 = $117

   Change the percent to a decimal and follow the interest formula (i = prt).

5. $640 The question asks you to multiply the principal ($8,000) by the rate (.08) by the time (1). $8,000 × .08 = $640.00 $640 × 1 = $640

EXERCISE 17B ――――――――――――――――――――――――――――――――

6. $26 $400 × .065 = $26.000 $26 × 1 = $26

7. $87.75 $900 × .0975 = $87.7500 $87.75 × 1 = $87.75

8. $495 $6,000 × .0825 = $495.0000 $495 × 1 = $495

9. $271.25 $3,500 × .775 = $271.2500 $271.25 × 1 = $271.25

   Change the percent to a decimal and follow the interest formula (i = prt).

10. $2,070 The question asks you to multiply the principal ($18,000) by the rate (.115) by the time (1). $18,000 × .115 = $2,070 $2,070 × 1 = $2,070

USE WHAT YOU HAVE LEARNED ――――――――――――――――――――――――

1. $96.25 $875 × .11 = 96.25 $96.25 × 1 = $96.25

2. $475 $9,500 × .05 = $475.00 $475 × 1 = $475

3. $12.60 $360 × .035 = $12.600 $12.60 × 1 = $12.60

4. $346.50 $4,200 × .0825 = $346.5000 $346.50 × 1 = $346.50

   Change the percent to a decimal and follow the interest formula (i = prt).

5. $390 The question asks you to multiply the principal ($6,500) by the rate (.06) by the time (1). $6,500 × .06 = $390.00 $390 × 1 = $390

6. $360 The question asks you to multiply the principal ($8,000) by the rate (.045) by the time (1). $8,000 × .045 = $360.000 $360 × 1 = $360

7. $193.75 The question asks you to multiply the principal ($1,250) by the rate (.155) by the time (1). $1,250 × .155 = $193.750 $193.75 × 1 = $193.75

8. $1,578.75 The question asks you to multiply the principal ($1,500) by the rate (.0525) by the time (1). Then add that answer ($78.75) to the original principal ($1,500). $1,500 × .0525 = $78.75 $1,500.00 + 78.75 = $1,578.75

9. The monthly payment will be $1,362.50. First multiply the principal ($15,000) by the rate (.09) by the time (1). Then add that answer ($1,350) to the original loan amount ($15,000). Then divide that total ($16,350) by the number of months (12). $15,000 × .09 × 1 = $1,350 $15,000 + $1,350 = $16,350 $16,350 ÷ 12 = $1,362.50

10. The monthly payment will be $1,135.00. First multiply the principal ($12,000) by the rate (.135) by the time (1). Then add to that answer ($1,620) the original loan amount ($12,000). Then divide that total ($13,620) by the number of months (12). $12,000 × .135 × 1= $1,620 $12,000 + $1,620 = $13,620 $13,620 ÷ 12 = $1,135

LESSON 18 Simple Interest for More Than a Year   pages 83-85

EXERCISE 18

1. $650 × .13 × 2

$650
×.13
1950
+6500
$84.50

$84.50
×2
$169.00

2. $8,000 × .065 × 5

$8,000
×.065
40000
+480000
520.000

$520
×5
$2,600

3. $13,000 × .09 × 4.5

$13,000
×.09
$1,170.00

$1,170
×4.5
5850
+46800
$5,265.0

4. $2,700 × .055 × 1.5

$2,700
×.055
13500
+13500
$148.500

$148.5
×1.5
7425
+14850
$222.750

Did you change the percent to a decimal? Did you follow the interest formula: i = prt?

5. $930 The question asks you to multiply the principal ($6,000) by the rate (.0775) by the time (2). $6,000 × .0775 × 2 = $930

1. $1,600 × .09 × 3.25

$1,600
×.09
$144.00

$144
×3.25
720
2880
+43200
$468.00

2. 950 × .0475 × 2

$950
×.0475
4750
66500
+380000
$45.1250

$45.125
×2
$90.25

3. $1,280 × .15 × 5.5

$1,280
×.15
6400
+12800
$192.00

$192
×5.5
960
+9600
$1,056.0

4. $1,400 × .07 × 4.75

$1,400
×.07
$98.00

$98
×4.75
490
6860
+39200
$465.50

5. $560 × .0325 × 1.5

$560
×.0325
2800
11200
+168000
$18.2000

$18.2
×1.5
910
+1820
$27.30

6. $18,000 × .115 × 8.5

$18,000
×.115
90000
180000
+1800000
$2,070.000

$2,070
×8.5
10350
+165600
$1,7595.0

Did you change the percent to a decimal? Did you follow the interest formula: i = prt?

7. $2,673.75 The question asks you to multiply the principal ($15,500) by the rate (.0575) by the time (3). $15,500 × .0575 × 3 = $2,673.75

8. $20.25 The question asks you to multiply the principal ($200) by the rate (.0675) by the time (1.5). $200 × .0675 × 1.5 = $20.25

9. The monthly payment will be $323.75. The question asks you to multiply the principal ($10,500) by the rate (.12) by the time (4). Then add that answer ($5,040) to the original principal ($10,500). Multiply 12 by 4 to find the number of months of payments there will be. Then divide the total ($15,540) by the number of months (48). $10,500 × .12 × 4 = $5,040 $10,500 + $5,040 = $15,500 $15,540 ÷ 48 = $323.75

10. $7,307.50 First subtract the down payment ($900) from the purchase price ($16,700). Then multiply the principal ($15,800) by the rate (.0925) by the time (5). $16,700 − $900 = $15,800 $15,800 × .0925 × 5 = $7,307.50

11. $27.00 The question asks you to multiply the principal ($400) by the rate (.045) by the time (1.5). $400 × .045 × 1.5 = $27.00

12. The monthly payment will be $377.00. First subtract the down payment ($550) from the purchase price ($9,250). Then multiply the principal ($8,700) by the rate (.12) by the time (2.5). Then add that number ($2,610) to the principal ($8,700). Multiply 12 months by 2.5. Then divide the total ($11,310) by the number of months (30). $9,250 − $550 = $8,700 $8,700 × .12 × 2.5 = $2,610 $8,700 + $2,610 = $11,310   12 × 2.5 = 30 $11,310 ÷ 30 = $377.00

LESSON 19 Simple Interest for Less Than a Year   pages 86-88

EXERCISE 19

1. $42.90 $\frac{6}{12} = \frac{1}{2}$ = .5 $780 × .11 = $85.80 $85.8 × .5 = $42.90

2. $97.50 $\frac{3}{12} = \frac{1}{4}$ = .25 $5,200 × .075 = $390.000 $390 × .25 = $97.50

3. $660 $\frac{9}{12} = \frac{3}{4}$ = .75 $11,000 × .08 = $880.00 $880 × .75 = $660.00

4. $56 $\frac{7}{12} = \frac{7}{12}$ $1,600 × .06 = $96.00 $\frac{\$96}{1} × \frac{7}{12} = \$56$

   Change the number of months to a decimal or a fraction, change the percent to a decimal, and follow the interest formula (i = prt).

5. $80 The question asks you to multiply the principal ($960) by the rate (.10) by the time $\left(\frac{5}{6}\right)$. $960 × .10 × \frac{5}{6} = \frac{\$96}{1} × \frac{5}{6} = \$80$

USE WHAT YOU HAVE LEARNED

1. $38 $\frac{4}{12} = \frac{1}{3}$ $1,900 × .06 = $114.00 $\frac{\$114}{1} × \frac{1}{3} = \$38$

2. $5.50 $\frac{6}{12} = \frac{1}{2}$ = .5 $400 × .0275 = $11.0000 $11 × .5 = $5.5

3. $44 $\frac{2}{12} = \frac{1}{6}$ $1,650 × .16 = $264.00 $\frac{\$264}{1} × \frac{1}{6} = \$44$

4. $60 $\frac{8}{12} = \frac{2}{3}$ $1,800 \times .05 = \$90.00$ $\frac{\$90}{1} \times \frac{2}{3} = \$60$

5. $50 $\frac{10}{12} = \frac{5}{6}$ $800 \times .075 = \$60.000$ $\frac{\$60}{1} \times \frac{5}{6} = \$50$

6. $500 $\frac{5}{12} = \frac{5}{12}$ $10,000 \times .12 = \$1,200.00$ $\frac{\$1,200}{1} \times \frac{5}{6} = \$500$

Change the number of months to a decimal or a fraction, change the percent to a decimal, and follow the interest formula (i = prt?).

7. $180.00 The question asks you to multiply the principal ($2,000) by the rate (.12) by the time (.75). $2,000 \times .12 \times .75 = \$180.00$

8. $30 The question asks you to multiply the principal ($900) by the rate (.08) by the time $\left(\frac{5}{12}\right)$. $\$900 \times .08 \times \frac{5}{12} = \frac{\$72}{1} \times \frac{5}{12} = \$30$

9. $12.60 The question asks you to multiply the principal ($360) by the rate (.07) by the time (.5). $360 \times .07 \times .5 = \$12.60$

10. The monthly payment will be $137.50. First subtract the down payment ($250) from the purchase price ($1,500). Then multiply the principal ($1,250) by the rate (.12) by the time $\left(\frac{5}{6}\right)$. Add that answer ($125) to the principal ($1,250) to get the total amount financed. Then divide that number ($1,375) by the number of months (10). $1,500 − $250 = $1,250 $1,250 \times .12 \times \frac{5}{6} = $125 $1,250 + $125 = $1,375 $1,375 ÷ 10 = $137.50

11. $324 The question asks you to multiply the principal ($320) by the rate (.05) by the time (.25). Then take that answer ($4) and add it to the principal ($320) to get the total. $320 \times .05 \times .25 = $4 $320 + $4 = $324

12. The monthly payment will be $826.00. First subtract the down payment ($300) from the purchase price ($3,500). Then multiply the principal ($3,200) by the rate (.0975) by the time $\left(\frac{1}{3}\right)$. Then add that number ($104) to the principal ($3,200). Then divide the total ($3,304) by the number of months (4). $3,500 − $300 = $3,200 $3,200 \times .0975 \times \frac{1}{3} = $104 $3,200 + $104 = $3,304 $3,304 ÷ 4 = $826.00

LESSON 20 Compound Interest   pages 89-92

EXERCISE 20A

1. $198.45 $180 \times .05 = $9.00 $180 + $9 = $189 $189 \times .05 = $9.45 $189.00 + $9.45 = $198.45

2. $1,297.92 $1,200 \times .04 = $48.00 $1,200 + $48 = $1,248 $1,248 \times .04 = $49.92 $1,248.00 + $49.92 = $1,297.92

3. $786.52 $700 × .06 = $42.00 $700 + $42 = $742 $742 × .06 = $44.52
$742.00 + $44.52 = $786.52

4. $445.21 $400 × .055 = $22.000 $400 + $22 = $422 $422 × .055 =
$23.210 $422.00 + $23.21 = $445.21

Find the interest for the first year, add that interest to the principal, and use
the new principal to find the interest for the second year

5. $572.45 The question asks you to find the interest rate for the first year: $500
× .07 × 1 = $35. Then add that answer ($35) to the original principal ($500).
Then take the new principal ($535) and find the interest rate for the second
year: $535 × .07 × 1 = $37.45; $535 + $37.45 = $572.45.

EXERCISE 20B

6. $324.48 $300 × .08 = $24.00 $24 × .5 = $12.0 $300 + $12 = $312 $312 ×
.08 = $24.96 $24.96 × .5 = $12.480 $312.00 + $12.48 = $324.48

7. $1,060.90 $1,000 × .06 = $60.00 $60 × .5 = $30.0 $1,000 + $30 = $1,030
$1,030 × .06 = $61.80 $61.8 × .5 = $30.90 $1,030.00 + $30.90 = $1,060.90

8. $832.32 $800 × .04 = $32.00 $32 × .5 = $16.0 $800 + $16 = $816 $816 ×
.04 = $32.64 $32.64 × .5 = $16.32 $816.00 + $16.32 = $832.32

9. $2,060.45 $2,000 × .03 = $60.00 $60 × .5 = $30.0 $2,000 + $30 = $2,030
$2,030 × .03 = $60.90 $60.9 × .5 = $30.45 $2,030 + $30.45 = $2,060.45

Find the interest for the first 6 months, add that interest to the principal,
and use the new principal to find the interest for the second 6 months.

10. $212.18 The question asks you to find the interest for the first 6 months:
$200 × .06 = $12.; $12 × .5 = $6. Add this amount ($6) to the original
principal ($200). Then take the new principal ($206) and find the interest for
the second 6 months: $206 × .06 = $6.18; $206 + $6.18 = $212.18.

USE WHAT YOU HAVE LEARNED

1. $641.52 $550 × .08 = $44.00 $550 + $44 = $594 $594 × .08 = $47.52
$594.00 + $47.52 = $641.52

2. $1,780.84 $1,600 × .055 = $88.000 $1,600 + $88 = $1,688 $1,688 × .055
= $92.840 $1,688.00 + $92.84 = $1,780.84

3. $104.04 $100 × .04 = $4.00 $4 × .5 = $2.0 $100 + $2 = $102 $102 × .04
= $4.08 $4.08 × .5 = $2.04 $102.00 + $2.04 = $104.04

4. $1,485.26 $1,400 × .06 = $84.00 $84 × .5 = $42.0 $1,400 + $42 = $1,442
$1,442 × .06 = $86.52 $86.52 × .5 = $43.26 $1,442.00 + $43.26 = $1,485.26

Find the interest for the first 6 months, add that interest to the principal,
and use the new principal to find the interest for the second 6 months.

5. $378.56 Find the interest for the first year: $350 × .04 = $14. Add that amount ($14) to the original principal ($350). Then take the new principal ($364), and find the interest for the second 6 months: $364 × .04 = $14.56; $364 + $14.56 = $378.56.

6. $291.60 Find the interest for the first 6 months: $250 × .08 = $20. Add that amount ($20) to the original principal ($250). Then take the new principal ($270) and find the interest for the second 6 months: $270 × .08 = $21.60; $270 + $21.60 = $291.60.

7. $114.49 Find the interest for the first year: $100 × .07 = $7. Add this amount ($7) to the original principal ($100). Then take the new principal ($107), and find the interest for the second year: $107 × .07 = $7.49; $107 + $7.49 = $114.49.

8. $2,226.05 Find the interest for the first year: $2,000 × .055 = $110. Add this amount ($110) to the original principal ($2,000). Then take the new principal ($2,110) and find the interest rate for the second year: $2,110 × .055 = $116.05; $2,110 + $116.05 = $2,226.05.

9. $486.72 First, divide $900 by 2. Take this amount ($450), and find the interest made for the first 6 months: $450 × .08 = $36; $36 ÷ 2 = $18. Add this amount ($18) to the original principal ($450). Then take the new principal ($468) and find the interest for the second 6 months: $468 × .08 = $37.44; $37.44 ÷ 2 = $18.72; $468 + $18.72 = $486.72.

10. 636.54 First, add all of Frank's commissions: $210 + $240 + $150 = $600. Take this amount ($600), and find the interest for the first 6 months: $600 × .06 = $36; 36 ÷ 2 = $18. Add this amount ($18) to the original principal ($600). Then take the new principal ($618), and find the interest for the second 6 months: $618 × .06 = $37.08; $37.08 ÷ 2 = $18.54; $618 + $18.54 = $636.54.

CHAPTER 4 Summary   pages 93-94

EXERCISE A

1. $24.00   i = prt i = 400 × .06 × 1 = 24

2. $28.50 i = prt i = 600 × .0475 × 1 = 28.5

3. $210.00   i = prt i = 4,000 × .0525 × 1 = 210

If you have trouble, refer to Lesson 17.

EXERCISE B

4. $218.75   i = prt i = 1,200 × .06 × 1.25 = 210

5. $90.00   i = prt i = 750 × .0575 × 2 = 90

6. $487.20   i = prt i = 1,160 × .12 × 3.5 = 487.20

7. $280.00   i = prt i = 1,700 × .06 × 2.75 = 280.5

If you have trouble, refer to Lesson 18.

8. $37.50 $i = prt$ $i = 1,500 \times .05 \times \dfrac{1}{2} = 37.5$

9. $5.10 $i = prt$ $i = 600 \times .034 \times \dfrac{1}{4} = 5.1$

10. $103.50 $i = prt$ $i = 1,150 \times .12 \times \dfrac{3}{4} = 103.5$

11. $9.60 $i = prt$ $i = 96 \times .15 \times \dfrac{2}{3} = 9.6$

If you have trouble, refer to Lesson 19.

12. $51.52 $i = prt$ $i = 45 \times .07 \times 1 = 3.15$ $45 + 3.15 = 48.15$ $i = prt$ $i = 48.15 \times .07 \times 1 = 3.3705$ $3.15 + 3.37 = 6.52 + 45 = 51.52$

13. $1,310.43 $i = prt$ $i = 1,200 \times .045 \times 1 = 54$ $1,200 + 54 = 1,254$ $i = prt$ $i = 1,254 \times .045 \times 1 = 56.43$ $54 + 56.43 = 110.43 + 1,200 = 1,310.43$

14. $1,485.26 $i = prt$ $i = 1,400 \times .06 \times \dfrac{1}{2} = 42$ $1,400 + 42 = 1,442$ $i = prt$ $i = 1,442 \times .06 \times \dfrac{1}{2} = 43.26$ $42 + 43.26 + 1,400 = 1,485.26$

15. $215.57 $i = prt$ $i = 200 \times .05 \times \dfrac{1}{2} = 5$ $200 + 5 = 205$ $i = prt$ $i = 205 \times .05 \times \dfrac{1}{2} = 5.125$, or 5.13 $205 + 5.13 = 210.13$ $i = prt$ $i = 210.13 \times .05 \times \dfrac{1}{2} = 5.25325$, or 5.25 $210.18 + 5.25 = 215.43$ $i = prt$ $i = 215.43 \times .05 \times \dfrac{1}{2} = 5.38575$, or 5.39. $210.18 + 5.39 = 215.57$

If you have trouble, refer to Lesson 20.

CHAPTER 4 Math at Work   pages 95-98

1. In one year they will earn $318.75 in interest.
   $I = PRT$
   $I = (\$8,500 \times 3\dfrac{3}{4}\% \times 1\text{year})$
   $3\dfrac{3}{4}\% = 3.75\% = .0375\%$
   $\$8,500 \times .0375 = \$318.75$
   $\$318.75 \times 1 = \$318.75$

2. In five years, the customer will pay $5,437.50 in simple interest.
   $I = PRT$
   $I = (\$16,500 - \$2,000) \times 7\dfrac{1}{2}\% \times 5$
   $I = (\$14,500) \times (7\dfrac{1}{2}\% = 7.5\% = .075) \times 5$
   $I = \$14,500 \times .075 \times 5$
   $I = \$1,087.50 \times 5$
   $I = \$5,437.50$

3. She will earn $153.13 in simple interest in one year.
I = PRT
I = $4,375. × 3.5% × 1
I = $4.375 × .035 × 1
I = $153.13 × 1
I = $153.13

4. He will earn more interest in the compounded interest CD.

Simple Interest Savings	Compound Interest CD
I = PRT	I = PRT
I = $2,000 × 3.5% × 1	I = $2,000 × 3.5% × .6
I = $2,000 × .035 × 1	I = $2,000 × .035 × .6
I = $70 × 1	I = $70 × .6
I = $70	I = $42
I = $42+ $2,000 × .035 × .6	
I = $2.042 × .035 × .6	
I = $71.47 × .6	
I = $1.50	
I = $2042. + $1.50 = $2,043.50	

5. They will pay $90.10 in interest.
I = PRT
I = $1,059.95 × 4.25% × 2
I = $1,059.95 × .0425 × 2
I = $ 45.05 × 2
I = $90.10

6. They will earn $100.14 by depositing the money for 6 months at 3.9% interest.
I = PRT
I = $5,135 × 3.9% × 6 months
I = $5,135 × .039 × .5 (year)
I = $ 200.27 × .5
I = $100.14

7. Their monthly payments were $230.91.
I = PRT
I = $2,599.95 − $500 × 12% × 10 months.
I = $2,099.95 × .12 × $\frac{10}{12}$
I = $251.99 × $\frac{10}{12}$ $\frac{10}{12}$ = .83
I = $251.99 × .83
I = $209.15

$$MP = \frac{P + I}{\text{\# of months}}$$

$$MP = \frac{\$2,099.95 + \$209.15}{10 \text{ months}}$$

$$MP = \frac{\$2,309.09}{10} \text{ months}$$

MP = $230.91(rounded to the nearest hundredth)

8. Phil will earn $73.50 if he puts his money in this account.

$I = PRT$

$I = \$1,500 \times 4.9\% \times 1$

$I = \$1,500 \times .049 \times 1$

$I = \$73.50 \times 1$

$I = \$73.50$

9. Clancy's company will not earn at least $100 in interest on savings.

$I = PRT$

$I = \$2,000 \times 4.75\% \times 1$

$I = \$2,000 \times .0475 \times 1$

$I = \$95.00 \times 1$

$I = \$95.00$

10. He will pay $287.5 in interest if he repays the loan in six months.

$I = PRT$

$I = \$5,000 \times 11.5\% \times (1 \times 6 \text{ months})$

$I = \$5,000 \times .115 \times (1 \times .5 \text{ year})$

$I = \$575. \times .5$

$I = \$287.5$

11. The total repayment is $7,685.63.

$I = PRT$

$I = \$7,500 \times 9.9\% \text{ per year} \times 3 \text{ months}$

$I = \$7,500 \times .099 \times .25 \text{ or one year}$

$I = 742.50 \times .25$

$I = \$185.63$

$I = \$7,500 + \$185.63 = \$7,685.63$

12. She withdrew $391.00.

$I = PRT$

$I = \$10,000 \times 4\frac{1}{4}\% \times 11 \text{ months}$

$I = \$10,000 \times .0425 \times \dfrac{11}{12}$

$I = \$425 \times .92$

$I = \$391$

13. Fred will earn more Interest in Bank B because the rate is higher. $4.5\% > 3.5\%$ whether it is compounded or not.

14. Balance at end of Second Quarter (6 months) is $6,135.76.

$I = PRT$

$I = \$6,000 \times 4.5\%(\text{per year}) \times .25 \text{ (First Quarter)}$

$I = \$6,000 \times .045 \times .25$

$I = \$67.50$

Balance at end of First Quarter (3 months) = $6,067.500

$I = \$6,067.50 \times 4.5\%(\text{per year}) \times .25 \text{ (Second Quarter)}$

$I = \$6,067.50 \times .045 \times .25$

$I = \$68.26$

15. Balance at end of second 6 months is $773.26.
P = $300 + $279. + $157 = $736
I = $736 × 5% (per year) × 6 months
I = $18.40
Balance at end of first 6 months = $736 + 18.40 = $754.40
I = $754.40 × 5% × 6 months
I = $18.86

16. The monthly payment is $108.78.
$2,335.99 × 10% = $233.60 down payment.
I = PRT
I = ($,2335.99 − $233.60) × 12% × 2
I = $2,105.39 × .12 × 2
I = $252.65 × 2
I = $505.30

$$MP = \frac{P + I}{\# \text{ months}}$$

$$MP = \frac{\$2,105.39 + \$505.30}{24 \text{ months}}$$

MP = $108.78

17. The monthly payment is $351.33.
$12,000 − $2,700 = $9300.00
I = PRT
I = $9,300 × 12% × 3 years
I = $9,300 × .12 × 3
I = $9,300 × .36
I = $3,348.

$$MP = \frac{P + I}{\# \text{ months}}$$

$$MP = \frac{\$9,300 + \$3,348.00}{36 \text{ months}}$$

MP = $351.33

18. They will have paid $83.83 in interest after three months.
$4,299.00 × 20% = $859.80
I = PRT
I = ($4,299. − $859.80) × $9\frac{3}{4}$% × 1
I = $3,439.20 × .0975 × 1
I = $335.32
3/12 = .25 (by paying early) × $335.32
I = $83.83

19. Ivan's Ice Cream Company will makes $150.
I = PRT
I = $1,000 × 3% × 1 year × 5 employees
I = $1,000 × .03 × 1 × 5
I = $30 × 1 × 5
I = $150.

20. The total Interest is $120.00.

        Family A =   0.   (They paid in full)

        Family B = $ 30. $3,000 × 2% × 6 months

                $3,000 × .02 × .5 years

                $30.

        Family C = $ 90. $6,000 × .03 × 1

                $6,000 × .03 × 1

                $90

21. $3,088.76

    I = PRT

    I = $1,000 × .05 × .25 years

    I = $12.50 First Quarter Interest

    P = $1,000 + $12.50 + deposit $500

    I = $1,512.50 × .05 × .25

    I = $18.91 Second Quarter Interest

    P = $1512.50 + 18.91 + deposit $500

    I = $2,031.41 × .05 × .25

    I = $25.39 Third Quarter Interest

    P = $2031.41 + $25.39 + deposit $500

    I = $2556.80 × .05 × .25

    I = $31.96 Forth Quarter Interest

    P = $2,556.80 + $31.96 + deposit $500

    Total at end of the year = $3,088.76

22. $88.76

    Original principal = $1,000

    Deposits + $2,000

    Balance − Total Principal = Interest

    $3,088.76 − $3,000.00 = $88.76

23. $10,875.00

    I = PRT

    I = $10,000 × 8.75% × 3 years

    I = $10,000 × .0875 × 3

    I = $875 × 3

    I = $2,625

    Total Cost = Purchase Price + Interest

    Total Cost = $10,000 + $875.00

    Total Cost = $10,875.00

24. $261.25

    I + PRT

    I = ($2,000 + $3,500) × 7% × 2 years

    I = $5,500 × .07 × 2

    I = $385.00 × 2

    I = $770

$$MP = \frac{P + I}{\# \text{ months}}$$

$$MP = \frac{\$5,500 + \$770}{24 \text{ months}}$$

    MP = $261.25